More Praise for *The Art of Astute Investing:*

"A sensible guide for non-experts, the book provides excellent advice on diversifying to reduce risk, minimizing expenses, and maximizing long-term returns."
—Stephen Brobeck, Executive Director, Consumer Federation of America

"This is a how-to book with a difference. It motivates the reader to establish an investment strategy. It is essential for anyone facing the financial burden of major life events—home, college, retirement, and succession."
—Richard M. Buxbaum, Dean, International and Area Studies, University of California, Berkeley

"I find Conover's insight into investing easy to understand and helpful to investors with any level of experience. A must-read for anyone considering investing in mutual funds."
—Richard L. Mount, President and CEO, Saratoga National Bank

"An excellent book for a family to use to guide its thinking about saving and investing, to help set its financial goals, and to make the investment choices required to build wealth."
—Robert H. Waterman, Jr., co-author of *In Search of Excellence* and author of *What America Does Right*

THE ART OF ASTUTE INVESTING

BUILDING WEALTH WITH No-LOAD MUTUAL FUNDS

C. TODD CONOVER

AMACOM

AMERICAN MANAGEMENT ASSOCIATION

NEW YORK • ATLANTA • BOSTON • CHICAGO • KANSAS CITY • SAN FRANCISCO • WASHINGTON, D.C.
BRUSSELS • MEXICO CITY • TOKYO • TORONTO

38485846
DLC

6-17-98

This book is available at a special
discount when ordered in bulk quantities.
For information, contact Special Sales Department,
AMACOM, a division of American Management Association,
1601 Broadway, New York, NY 10019.

Library of Congress Cataloging-in-Publication Data

Conover, C. Todd.
    The art of astute investing : building wealth with no-load mutual
funds / C. Todd Conover.
        p.   cm.
    Includes bibliographical references and index.
    ISBN 0-8144-0406-5
    1. Mutual funds.   I. Title.
HG4530.C59   1998
332.63'27—dc21   98-5918
                                                    CIP

Printing number

10   9   8   7   6   5   4   3   2   1

To my wife, **Sally,** and our daughters, **Kirsten** and **Alison.** They provided the reason to manage our family's financial affairs in a sensible way and the motivation to pass on some knowledge to others who might benefit.

Thanks for the encouragement and for putting up with me while I was writing this book.

CONTENTS

EXHIBITS

PREFACE

Most books about investing are long and descriptive. They explain the nature of stocks, bonds, and mutual funds; how stock exchanges and brokers work; how bond prices respond to changes in interest rates; and so forth. These books inform and educate, but they do not help investors actually make investment decisions.

This book is intended to overcome that weakness and fill a much-needed void. It's a short, how-to book for individual investors. It guides investors through the process of developing and implementing a savings and investment program.

The four most important events in the financial lives of most people are buying a house, sending children to college, retirement, and, possibly, leaving an estate to their heirs. The book will help determine how much money you will need for each event and how large an investment portfolio you must accumulate to meet those needs.

Mutual funds are the best investments for building your portfolio. They provide instant diversification, professional management, and liquidity. You should invest only in no-load funds—those without up-front or deferred sales charges. Why? There are lots of them to choose from. They perform as well as or better than funds on which a typical 4 to 6 percent sales load is charged. And there is no need to incur an avoidable expense that represents a significant part of a year's investment return.

You need only three tools to develop your mutual fund portfolio: a subscription to *Morningstar No-Load Funds;* an account with Charles Schwab & Co., Fidelity Investments, or the Vanguard

Group; and the Sunday edition of the *New York Times*. The book explains the role of each tool and how to use them.

After determining how much money you need, you will be guided through the decision-making process. To aid in this task, I use a hypothetical investor I call the Smith family. As they develop their portfolio, you will develop yours. You will see how to (1) portray your present financial situation, (2) allocate assets among equities, fixed income securities, and cash reserves, and (3) select a small number of funds to achieve diversification, a tolerable level of risk, and a good return on investment. You will also learn what you can do to minimize your income tax burden in the aftermath of the 1997 tax law.

The book also helps you develop an implementation plan. The plan format accommodates new savings, as well as rebalancing your portfolio to maintain the desired asset mix. When appropriate, it includes a schedule of how much to invest in each fund every month. In addition, you will learn how to monitor performance and when to make adjustments to your portfolio. Knowing when to sell is just as important as the decision to buy a particular fund.

The best way to use this book is to read it once to get an overall understanding of what it's all about. Then read it again in more detail, and review the exhibits carefully. They are easy to follow, and you may use some of them as worksheets.

Investing involves making choices. I use specific mutual funds to illustrate how to make certain choices. "The Conover Short List of Great No-Load Mutual Funds," shown in an appendix, contains my recommended funds. The book provides a way for you to select the funds that are best for you. Most investors will probably want to go through the process more than once: make an initial selection, inspect the results, and do it again until they get it right. And getting it right is a matter of judgment. This book provides a framework for applying that judgment.

Comments and suggestions on how to improve this book and make it more helpful and user-friendly to individual investors are most welcome. They should be addressed to:

C. Todd Conover
The Vantage Group
101 First Street, Suite 670
Los Altos, California 94022

(650) 961-1400
Fax: (650) 254-1314
E-mail: tconover@aol.com

Have a good time, and make good investment choices.

Acknowledgments

Lots of friends helped me with this book. Some read drafts and called with suggestions. Others wrote notes or sent e-mail messages. Most readers don't care who they are or what contribution they made, so most readers can skip this page. But I care. Thus, the real purpose of this page is for me to thank those who helped me and to get their names in print.

The earliest readers included Bob White, a partner at Edgar, Dunn & Company, and David Chew, who worked with me in the Office of the Comptroller of the Currency and then served as deputy assistant to the president in the Reagan administration. Both read the entire draft and all the exhibits several times. They gave me detailed reactions and suggestions for improvement. Their ideas helped me shape the book and make it more useful to individual investors.

My sister, Jo Carol Conover, asked that I write something about why people ought to save and invest in the first place. Doyle Arnold, an executive vice president at the Bank of America, made sure that I dealt with the impact of income taxes. Dave Poe, another partner at Edgar, Dunn & Company, asked me to discuss several retirement topics. Brian Smith, a partner with the law firm of Mayer, Brown & Platt in Washington, D.C., told me such a book was much needed by lawyers everywhere.

Investment professionals who contributed include Morgan White, of Woodside Asset Management; Norm Boone, of Boone & Associates; Katie Cattanach, of Sovereign Financial Services; Paul Solli from Financial Design; and Bo Cornell, of Dimensional Fund

Advisors. David Pottruck, the president of Charles Schwab & Co., and Barbara Heinrich, senior vice president, reviewed the book and introduced me to several investment advisers so that I could get their perspective.

Mary Bush, John Ferneborg, George Glaser, David Gregory, Claude Hutchison, Richard Ives, Dick Kraber, Roger McGee, Mike Moore, Conrad Prusak, Harvey Rowen, John Twomey, Ray Williams, and John Woods all reviewed at least one draft and gave me valuable feedback. My apologies to anyone I've forgotten.

Lucinda Lee, my talented estate planning attorney, and Sandra L. Collins, my very able tax accountant for many years, both reviewed the book with their specialties in mind to make sure I was on track. My literary agent, Wendy Keller, of the ForthWrite Literary Agency, liked the book right away, recommended some improvements, and worked with enthusiasm to find an outstanding publisher.

My special thanks to Don Phillips, the president of Morningstar, and his colleagues for their excellent publications and for sharing some of their thoughts and perspectives with me. Thanks also to the *New York Times*, the *Wall Street Journal*, Ibbotson Associates, Charles Schwab & Co., Fidelity Investments, and the Vanguard Group for the information they provide that helps individual investors make investment decisions.

All of these people and organizations contributed to the content and message of the book. Thanks to all of them for caring and for helping. It has taken more time than I originally envisioned, but writing this book has been a great experience for me. Of course, I bear full responsibility for the results.

1

GETTING STARTED

You have got to be an investor. Whatever your business or profession, investing should be your second job. It is not hard to do. All it takes is understanding, commitment, and a little effort. But it is worth the effort. By practising the art of astute investing, you can achieve financial independence—the ability to do whatever you want without being dependent on somebody else.

When I say "astute," I mean thoughtful, intelligent, logical, analytical, clever—even shrewd. In the world of investing, knowing the answers to some fundamental questions and adhering to some basic principles can make you astute. When you know the facts and understand the numbers, you can make astute investment decisions. You also need an investment philosophy to serve as the foundation for your investment activities. Since you may not have one yet, I am going to share mine with you.

Today's investment environment demands your attention. The future of social security is uncertain. Traditional pension plans are being de-emphasized and replaced by 401(k) plans, in which employees are expected to put up most of their own retirement money and then to decide how to invest it. People all over America, led by the baby boomers, are hearing the wake-up call. They know that nobody will look after their financial future unless they take some responsibility for it themselves. As a result, they are pouring money into the stock market in record amounts. At the same time, many of them want to play a more active role in investment decisions rather than relying entirely on someone else to do it for them.

Under the Taxpayer Relief Act of 1997, the capital gains tax has been cut to 20 percent. New and current individual retirement accounts (IRAs) have expanded eligibility and permit withdrawals without penalty for education and first-time home purchases. Homeowners may exclude gains of up to $500,000 on the sale of their primary residences, thus eliminating taxes on home sales for the vast majority of Americans. The estate tax exclusion increases from $600,000 in 1997 to $625,000 in 1998, and gradually to $1 million in 2006. These changes leave more money in the hands of taxpayers and make saving and investing more attractive to them in their role as individual investors.

In the 1980s and 1990s the U.S. stock markets have boomed. Charles Schwab & Co., Fidelity Investments, and Vanguard Group have become household words. Banks are selling mutual funds. There has been an information explosion. The *Wall Street Journal, Forbes, Fortune, Money, Worth,* and *Smart Money* all provide extensive coverage on mutual fund performance. CNBC and CNN provide news, analysis, and commentary on market and economic developments all day long. Numerous sites on the World Wide Web provide stock market information and investment advice. With the Internet, we can track our investments and initiate transactions 24 hours a day, 7 days a week.

Individual investors can thrive in the new world of information and technology. The tools are there to help you become an astute, well-informed investor. All you must do is learn to use them. This book is one of the tools. It provides a logical approach to saving and investing. It focuses on how to develop an investment portfolio—that is, a collection of no-load mutual funds that provide diversification and produce an attractive return on investment. It will satisfy your need for results and your tolerance for risk. It works, and I feel confident about it. You will, too. If you use an independent investment adviser, this book will help you become a more effective partner with him or her in managing your portfolio.

Investing involves evaluating alternatives and making choices. You will be better off making explicit choices, with as much knowledge as possible, rather than implicit ones. Doing nothing is really making a decision—a decision that your current investment portfolio, whatever its size and composition, will meet your needs. Many people do nothing even though they think their portfolio is inadequate. They fail to act because they do not know what to do. This book shows you what to do.

Your first task is to specify your financial goals and determine how much you must save and invest to achieve them. Then, using readily available information and a step-by-step approach, you will make the investment choices required to build and maintain your portfolio. This approach works whether you are starting from scratch or want to reassess and challenge the approach that you, or your investment adviser, now use. It will enable you to structure your portfolio and choose its components. It is sensible because it provides a commonsense, analytically based approach to savings and investment decisions—just what astute investors want.

THE INVESTOR MAJORITY

The Investor Majority is not an exclusive club. Its members probably number in the millions. They are the vast silent majority of America's individual investors. They range in age from about 25 to 65 years old or more. They are men and women, married and single, with and without children. They include accountants, bankers, computer wizards, doctors and nurses, engineers, farmers, government employees, homemakers, lawyers, managers, pilots, salespeople, secretaries, teachers, and union members—a cross-section of America.

They are not speculators looking for a quick return. Their investment time horizon is at least 5 years, and preferably longer. Their financial goals most likely include buying a home, sending a child or grandchild to college, ensuring a financially secure retirement for themselves, or leaving an estate to their heirs.

They are neither investment experts nor absolute beginners. They already own some common stocks or mutual funds. They have some investment experience, such as selecting investments for their IRA accounts or 401(k) plans. Regardless of their investment results, they are likely to lack confidence in their investment skills and be uncomfortable with the way they have made investment decisions. In short, they are frustrated with their experience as investors, and they want to do a better job of investing.

All of them have some money to invest—enough so that it is

important to invest wisely and earn an attractive return. Even if they understand that they must take more risk in order to earn higher returns, they are likely to be risk averse. They find it difficult to take the risks required to achieve the returns they want. This risk aversion adds to their frustration.

They have watched the raging bull market of the 1980s and 1990s and wished that they were more certain about how to invest and that they had more invested in equities. At present, they may be nervous about the market's level and future direction.

Many have neglected their savings and investment programs and feel the need to catch up. They want to learn more about investing, and they want help. They want to play a larger role in investment decisions or at least be able to have more intelligent discussions with their investment advisers.

They are uncomfortable with brokers who don't know anything about their financial situation and goals and want to sell them the investment that generates the highest commission. They mistrust the glossy material and grandiose claims set out in many investment newsletters. They want a commonsense approach that is based on logical principles and uses readily available information and understandable techniques.

As busy as they are with their careers and their families, they are willing to do some work to get good results. They expect to spend some concentrated time to get started and then devote a few days a year to make sure they are on track. The problem is that they are unsure about what steps to take and how to begin. This book tells you. It guides you through the entire decision-making process with explanations and examples. If you are part of the Investor Majority, this approach is for you.

EXPERIENCE AND RESULTS

I have been a frugal spender, a successful saver, and a frustrated investor for most of my adult life. For many years I was frustrated by the lack of good information on which to base investment decisions and the piecemeal approach to choosing investments. I wanted a comprehensive investment program with a clear picture of what I was trying to accomplish and what the composition of my investment portfolio should be. That way, I could make individual buy and sell decisions with confidence and within the context of an overall plan.

Nothing satisfied my needs until I discovered Morningstar. Its publications provided the information I needed about mutual funds. For the first time, I could clearly identify the similarities and differences among mutual funds. I could find in one place the information I needed to develop a portfolio of mutual funds, and it was presented in a consistent manner and updated periodically.

Using Morningstar's information, I developed and started using the approach described in this book. Since then, my results have been excellent. Even with a conservative asset mix, the value of my overall portfolio has more than doubled over the past 5 years. Obviously, I have benefited from a great bull market. My equity investments earned an excellent return compared to the Standard & Poor's (S&P) 500 Index, and I've maintained a more diversified portfolio and thus taken less risk. In spite of these results, I promise no outrageous returns in the future. You would probably be skeptical if I did. Nevertheless, you can do as well. This book tells you how.

I use this approach to manage my own portfolio and to advise on the portfolios of several other people. They include a 44-year-old surgeon, a 35-year-old single parent with $400,000 in investments, three couples with portfolios in the $200,000 to $500,000 range, and a 75-year-old widower with a portfolio of over $2.5 million. Their results, based in each case on an overall plan that they understand and are comfortable with, have also been excellent.

A number of interested friends and former colleagues have reviewed my approach. They include a partner in a Washington, D.C., law firm, a vice president of a major insurance company, and a senior management consultant. I've also tested my approach on several other investment advisers. All of them give it high marks for logic, simplicity, and sound analytical underpinnings.

ABOUT NUMBERS

One friend who reviewed the book commented that my approach sometimes seemed like an exercise in arithmetic. I was pleased with his remark. After all, investing is about numbers. If you don't want to understand and deal with numbers, you may conclude that do-it-yourself investing is not for you. You may be right. Nevertheless, you should still learn enough to be able to have an intelligent discussion with your investment adviser.

Whether you like numbers or not, and even if investing makes you uncomfortable, you face some important investment choices. For example, you probably have to decide how to invest the funds in your IRA or 401(k) account. Thus, it is hard to escape the need and responsibility for making at least a few investment decisions and for dealing with numbers. If you know the numbers, it's fairly easy to be astute. In that case, knowledge really is power.

If I can make investing in mutual funds as logical and straightforward as arithmetic, I will have helped you, and I will have succeeded in my goal of developing a useful tool for individual investors. Throughout the text and in the exhibits, I have often rounded numbers to the nearest $100 or $1,000 for ease of presentation. Since much of the book is about planning for the future, it isn't necessary to be more precise.

BASIC QUESTIONS FACING INVESTORS

Where should I put my money? That is the basic choice facing all investors. Naturally, different investors have different answers to that important question. They often rely on a particular investment approach or philosophy to guide their decisions. Such guiding principles are usually grounded in the investor's education, beliefs, or experience. The approach espoused in this book is no exception. It's based on my personal experience as an investor and private investment adviser.

Other fundamental questions also come to mind, about the investor's motivation, inflation, bias for or against certain types of investments, diversification, and taxes. My answers to these questions are part of the long-term investment philosophy and approach that I think should guide the activities of most individual investors.

WHY SAVE AND INVEST?

Everybody ought to have a good job and a savings and investment program. First, you should meet your needs for life, health, disability, and liability insurance and pay off any high-interest debt, such as credit card balances. Then you should focus on savings and building your investment portfolio.

To save is to set aside a portion of your current income that you will not spend now but will put to work to earn additional income. *To invest* is to buy assets such as mutual funds that, through a combination of interest, dividends, or capital appreciation, are expected to increase in value over time. Thus, an amount saved and invested wisely should grow to an even larger amount in the future.

If you have a lot of money, you ought to invest it wisely to earn an attractive return. To aim for less would be to waste some of the earning power of your assets. You could use that earning power to benefit yourself and others. If you have very little money, you should adopt a savings program that will enable you to accumulate wealth over time. Why? Because most of us face future financial needs that we will not be able to meet out of our current income. You may need to save and invest for the down payment on a house in 3 to 5 years, for college tuition in 12 to 18 years, and for retirement in 10 to 40 years. These are big expenses, and you will need lots of money to pay for them.

WHAT'S THE IMPACT OF INFLATION?

Inflation simply means that prices are increasing. If something that you bought for $1.00 last year now costs $1.04, that is 4 percent inflation. Since 1927, inflation has averaged 3.2 percent per year. From 1979 through 1981 it averaged 11.5 percent, and from 1991 through 1996, it averaged only 2.9 percent. In 1997, it was 1.7 percent.

We all hear a lot about inflation. The Bureau of Labor Statistics measures it via the Consumer Price Index (CPI), and the Federal Reserve Board (the Fed) tries to minimize and control it through monetary policy. During the 1990s, the Fed has increased rates on several occasions to try to slow a rapidly growing economy with inflationary tendencies. Higher interest rates hurt businesses that are trying to make a profit. As a result, the stock and bond markets generally react badly to evidence of increased inflation.

Inflation is bad because it erodes the purchasing power of your earnings. If your salary grows at less than the rate of inflation, you must work longer to be able to purchase the same goods and services. The ultimate result is that your standard of living will decline. Inflation is especially hard on older citizens who may be living on a fixed income.

Inflation also reduces the value of your financial assets: stocks, bonds, and cash reserves. If these investments earn less than the inflation rate, their purchasing power will also decline. If your investment returns only match the increase in the CPI, you are not making progress. However, if your investments earn 8 percent and inflation is 4 percent, then your real return is 4 percent, and you are increasing your wealth in real terms.

Real returns can be positive or negative. You must beat inflation and earn a positive real return in order to benefit from your investments. Thus, overcoming inflation is one of the strongest reasons for investing and taking the risks required to earn an attractive return on investment.

Why Mutual Funds?

One of my first investment choices is to focus on mutual funds. I believe that the investment portfolio for most individual investors should consist almost entirely of mutual funds rather than individual stocks, bonds, precious metals, futures, options, or real estate properties.

In recent years, mutual funds have become very popular with individual investors. Today there are more than 6,000 different mutual funds of all types: stock, bond, and money market funds. According to the Investment Company Institute (ICI), the trade association for mutual fund companies, an estimated 63 million individual Americans in 37 million U.S. households owned mutual fund shares at the end of 1996.

A 1995 ICI survey found that "the average mutual fund investor is middle class, 44 years old, has financial assets of $50,000, and is likely to be married and employed." Those households that purchased their first fund shares in 1990 or earlier owned three mutual funds and had median financial assets of $70,000, including $25,000 in mutual funds. By year-end 1996, Americans had 151 million mutual fund accounts with net assets of $3.5 trillion. The average account size was $23,400.

I focus on mutual funds because I believe that those of us who are not full-time investment professionals cannot know enough about the affairs of individual companies to make wise decisions regarding their securities. We certainly cannot know enough about enough companies to develop a diversified portfolio. Moreover, today there is excellent objective information about mutual fund behavior, performance, and risk. It makes sense to take advantage of this information to select the funds that will meet our objectives and provide appropriate diversification.

A portfolio of only five mutual funds with different investment objectives and styles could easily represent an investment in the stocks and bonds of 500 to 1,000 different companies. Thus, mutual funds are attractive because they provide instant diversification, professional asset management at a reasonable cost, automatic reinvestment of dividends, and *liquidity* (the ability to convert back to cash with a simple telephone call at any time).

WHY NO-LOAD FUNDS?

A true no-load mutual fund has no up-front sales charge or commission, no redemption fee, and no 12b-1 distribution fee (see the Glossary). Funds with 12b-1 fees of 0.25 percent of assets or less may also call themselves no-load funds. These charges directly reduce your return on investment. I choose no-load mutual funds because I see no reason why anyone should pay the typical sales charge of 4 to 6 percent of an investment if he or she can buy an equally good fund without any load. A 5 percent load takes $500 right off the top of a $10,000 investment. Your earnings base is then only $9,500. Depending on the market's performance, that 5 percent load could be a significant part of a fund's annual return. It could take a year or more just to earn the $500 back.

If you hold a fund for a long time, a 5 percent load may seem insignificant, but you also lose the earnings on the $500 for the life of the investment. At an 8 percent annual return, your $500 would grow to nearly $1,100 in 10 years and to more than $2,300 in 20 years. Moreover, if you should need to sell the fund in a short time, say, 3 years, you are more likely to incur a loss with a load fund than with a no-load fund. You have to earn the load back before you can break even. Finally, there is no evidence that annual operating expenses of no-load funds are higher than load funds. Regardless of what a commissioned stockbroker may tell you, you should stick to no-load funds.

WHY AND HOW TO DIVERSIFY?

Your portfolio should be broadly *diversified:* comprising assets whose values fluctuate independently of one another. That is, while some are increasing in value, others may be growing at different rates, holding constant, or even declining in value. The overall result is a smoothing of the peaks and valleys, which means a less volatile and thus less risky portfolio. You are more likely to get a good night's sleep if your portfolio is diversified than if it is concentrated in assets with the same or similar characteristics.

One very effective way to diversify is to own a *small* number of mutual funds that own a *large* number of different equity and fixed income securities. The funds should be run by different investment managers. That way, your portfolio's performance will not be too dependent on the results of any one fund, manager, industry, or company. For this reason most equity mutual funds own stock in at least 100 different companies. Most mutual funds also have limits on the percentage of the fund's assets that may be invested in any one company.

But there is more to diversification than just numbers. A portfolio with a small number of holdings may be more diversified than one with a large number of assets that are all affected by economic changes in the same way. A diversified portfolio should contain both stocks and bonds, international and domestic equities, different regional and country exposure, large and small companies, value- and growth-oriented firms, and securities with different levels of interest rate sensitivity. It should also include different industry sectors, such as utilities, energy, financial companies, consumer durables, services, retail, health, and technology. In short, you should achieve diversification by choosing mutual funds with different investment characteristics.

WHAT ABOUT INCOME TAXES?

Every investor's goal should be to earn an attractive *after-tax* return on investment. Success is measured not by how much you earn but by how much you can keep after the tax collector has taken his bite. Thus, income taxes have a major influence on investment decisions. The 20 percent federal capital gains tax rate for assets held 18 months or more definitely favors long-term investors. It increases the attractiveness of mutual funds that generate capital gains over those that pay dividends taxable at ordinary rates.

Mutual fund performance is reported on a pretax basis. Investors must make their own adjustments to determine their after-tax returns. To overcome this difficulty, with few exceptions I assume that all percentage returns are after applicable income taxes. Put another way, in some instances I assume that pretax returns and after-tax returns are the same.

This simplification works if you (1) reinvest interest and dividends and (2) pay state and federal income taxes on investment income out of your salary, both highly desirable practices. If possible, all investors should adopt them. In this way, the taxable part of your portfolio will grow as if it were held in a tax-advantaged account, such as an IRA, 401(k), or Keogh plan. It will grow to a larger amount since no withdrawals or tax payments will be taken out. Paying the taxes out of your earned income may become difficult as your portfolio grows and generates significant taxable income compared to your salary. Other tax-related issues, such as what type of funds to buy and which funds to hold in taxable and tax-deferred accounts, are dealt with in Chapters 4 and 6.

An Astute Approach

My approach begins by helping you establish your financial goals. It will then help you make the investment choices and decisions required to develop an investment portfolio that will suit your temperament and meet your needs. It features a hypothetical investor, three basic tools, and Seven Steps to a Sensible Portfolio.

A Hypothetical Investor

Throughout the book I use a hypothetical investor to illustrate how to develop and implement a savings and investment program. My hypothetical investor is the Smith family: Bill (age 45), Bonnie (age 42), and their son, Chris (age 8). Bill's annual salary is $42,000, and Bonnie earns $30,000, for a combined family income of $72,000.

Both of their employers provide a 401(k) plan in which an employee may contribute up to 15 percent of his or her salary, subject to the overall dollar limitation—$10,000 in 1998. The employers match employee contributions with 50 cents for each dollar up to 6 percent of the employee's salary. The Smiths both have IRAs. They also have residential real estate worth $225,000 and an investment portfolio of $120,000. Their current net worth is $175,000. A profile of the Smith family is shown in Exhibit 1-1. It is a snapshot of their family circumstances, including their income levels, applicable tax rates, financial objectives, and current assets. See if you can create a similar profile of your own family without looking through your files. Don't be concerned if you cannot; you will be able to soon.

The Smiths are doing well. In 1996, the median household income for married couples was almost $50,000. The top 20 percent of all households had income of more than $68,000, and the top 5 percent earned more than $119,000. Thus, the Smiths' income puts them in the top 20 million of America's 101 million households.

No doubt your situation is different from the Smiths'. You may be older or younger. Your income, obligations, investment portfolio, and net worth may be different from theirs. You may earn about the same amount as one of them or both of them combined, or your household income may be $100,000 or $200,000 or consider-

Exhibit 1-1. Profile of a hypothetical investor: The Smith family.

William A. Smith and Bonnie J. Smith
615 Marmaduke Way
Los Altos, California 94024
	Life event goals:
	    Public college for Chris in 10 years
	    Retirement in 20 years

Ages: Bill, 45; Bonnie, 42	Investment objective: Long-term growth
Children: Christopher, age 8	

Employment:
    Bill: Marketing director
    Bonnie: Store manager
	Tolerance for price fluctuation: Moderate

Adequate life, health, disability, and liability insurance	Annual income:
	    Bill: $42,000
	    Bonnie: $30,000

Residential real estate
    Current value: $225,000
    Purchase price: $200,000
	401(k) retirement plans:
	    Bill: 50% match to 6% of salary
	    Bonnie: 50% match to 6% of salary

Other assets: $85,000	IRA accounts: Bill and Bonnie

Investment portfolio: $120,000	Marginal income tax rates:
	    Federal: 28.0%
	    State: 8.0%
	    Combined: 33.8%

Total assets: $360,000	
	Federal capital gains tax rate: 20.0%
	Net worth: $175,000

ably more. Regardless of your financial situation, you probably share some of the same concerns about your financial future. Thus, the approach used for the Smiths applies to you too.

By following the exhibits, you will be able to trace the development of the Smiths' savings and investment program and use the approach to develop your own. Many of the exhibits are linked so that you can see the logical progression from one exhibit to the next. In fact, the exhibits are a vital part of the book. Be sure to review them carefully to ensure that you fully understand and thus will get the benefits of this approach.

THE THREE REQUIRED TOOLS

Investors today are bombarded by books, magazines, newsletters, newspaper articles, and investment-oriented Web sites. Articles with titles like, "The Only Six Funds You'll Need for This Year," offer advice without knowing anything about your needs. Many of them offer conflicting advice. For now, you can safely ignore all of this material. *After* your portfolio has been developed, you may want to read selectively over time to increase your knowledge and gain additional perspective.

Faced with information overload, it is easy for investors to get confused. Thus, another of my early investment choices was to simplify the information and record-keeping problem by using only three basic tools to help make investment decisions: (1) *Morningstar No-Load Funds,* a publication that costs $45 for a three-month trial and $175 for an annual subscription, (2) an account with Charles Schwab, Fidelity, or Vanguard, and (3) the Sunday edition of the *New York Times.* Each tool plays an important role.

Morningstar No-Load Funds provides a system for classifying and evaluating funds, performance data, and analysis of individual funds. It comes in two sections. The 24-page Summary Section contains articles of interest to investors, benchmark data, information on top and bottom performers, and an index with performance data of all funds the publication covers. The Analysis Section, comprising about 175 pages, contains overviews of the fund categories included in each issue and one-page analyses of individual funds. Since the publication includes funds with loads of 3 percent or less, as well as those with 12b-1 fees, you should be alert to the fees associated with each fund.

Schwab and Fidelity both offer a large selection of no-load mutual funds without any transaction fees; Vanguard charges a $35 service fee for each non-Vanguard fund order. All three firms provide trading by personal computer or touch-tone telephone, around-the-clock customer service, and comprehensive monthly statements.

Every Sunday, the *New York Times* provides up-to-date information on mutual fund performance using the same fund categories and rating system as Morningstar.

This book combines these three ingredients into an investment process for individual investors. You provide the brain power to make the process work.

Exhibit 1-2. Seven steps to a sensible portfolio.

1. **Set Financial Goals.** Determine how much money you will need and when you will need it for major life events: buying a house, sending a child to college, enjoying a comfortable retirement, or leaving an estate to your heirs. Prepare a brief summary of your goals.

2. **Determine Portfolio Mix.** Prepare an Investor's Balance Sheet to define your current financial position. Establish your asset allocation targets—the percentage of your portfolio that should be invested in equities, fixed income securities, and cash equivalent assets—and specify the basic composition of the equity portion.

3. **Choose Stock Fund Characteristics.** Specify the portion of your portfolio to be invested in value, blend, and growth funds and in funds that invest in large, medium, and small companies. Choose the characteristics of the funds that you want to own, including their ratings, basic features, operating expense levels, tax efficiency, degree of risk, and return on investment.

4. **Pick Mutual Funds.** Screen 4- and 5-star funds against the selection criteria; choose your stock funds, bond funds, and a money market fund; summarize your choices on a single page.

5. **Minimize Income Taxes.** Understand the basics of the 1997 tax law and the impact of taxes on investment decisions and performance; adopt strategies for the taxable and tax-advantaged portions of your portfolio.

6. **Implement, Monitor, and Adjust.** Develop an implementation plan and invest a constant amount each month to get the benefits of dollar cost averaging; monitor the performance of your portfolio and its components, and adjust your holdings to reflect changes in future outlook.

7. **Stay Astute.** Take steps to preserve your estate; keep key messages in mind as you invest for the future; and continue to read and learn about mutual fund investing.

SEVEN STEPS TO A SENSIBLE PORTFOLIO

By using the approach explained in this book, you will develop a sensible investment portfolio—one that is logical, practical, and reliable. It will be based on conservative assumptions. Since it will be well diversified, it should not earn the spectacular returns *or* suffer the huge losses often produced by a more concentrated portfolio. When you tell your friends about your portfolio, they will recognize that you are an astute investor.

The process used to build the portfolio is logical and easy to understand. First, you establish your financial goals. Then you develop a savings and investment program, including an investment portfolio, that will enable you to achieve them. The effort involves the seven steps shown in Exhibit 1-2. The remaining chapters of the book deal with these steps.

You start by taking inventory of your current investments, assessing the results, and determining the target mix for your assets in the future. You then evaluate funds against your choice of selection criteria and pick five to ten stock and bond mutual funds to give you a diversified portfolio. You adopt strategies to minimize your tax burden. Finally, you will see how to implement your decisions and adjust your portfolio to changing conditions. After you've mastered the seven steps, you can take the last step: relax and enjoy it. You will have confidence that your investment portfolio is in good hands—yours!

2

SETTING FINANCIAL GOALS

Many books and articles on personal financial planning urge the development of financial goals, and this book is no exception. Establishing financial goals makes good sense. To develop a savings and investment program, you must know how much money you will need and when you'll need it. The old adage is true: If you don't know where you're going, you can't chart a course to take you there.

So what are your financial goals? Pundits say you should know, and their logic is persuasive. But nobody tells you how to figure out what your goals should be or how you should use them once they are established. Well, this chapter tells you how.

Your financial goals should be linked to major life events: marriage, the purchase of a home, the birth of a child, the child's departure for college, your retirement, and even the potential death of you and/or your spouse. You can probably think of other events specific to your situation.

How much do you need to save? Many investors, especially baby boomers, seem to regard the answer to this question as their principal financial goal. Certainly it is an important question, but its answer really involves the resolution of at least four other questions. In life event terms, the concerns of many individual investors are:

- How much must we save for the down payment on a house or for another major expenditure?
- Are we saving enough to pay for our child's college education?
- What must we do to ensure that we will be financially comfortable during our retirement years?
- How, and to what extent, should we provide for our heirs?

Your answers to these questions may be converted into statements of financial goals. The statements should be unambiguous. Whenever possible, they should include a dollar amount and a time horizon—for example, "to build a college fund of $75,000 over the next 16 years." Once developed, they need not be etched in stone. In fact, you should review them annually and adjust them to fit changes in your circumstances.

You can answer the four questions by applying judgment and using the arithmetic of compound interest. The information you need to help answer the questions for yourself is contained in the exhibits.

SAVE TO BUY A HOUSE

If you are looking forward to making a down payment on a new residence or a vacation home, or if a new car or boat or other major expenditure is on the horizon, you may need to accumulate a sizable sum during the next few years. For example, to accumulate $25,000 in a taxable account over the next 4 years, you must save $470 per month, invest it at 5 percent, reinvest any interest or dividends, and pay any income taxes out of your salary.

Use the table in Exhibit 2-1 to determine the amount needed for other target amounts, time horizons, and interest rates. Start by picking when you will need the money—for example, in 4 years. Then choose the annual rate you believe you can earn in a safe investment, like a Treasury bill or a money market fund—say, 5 percent. You will find the amount you must save and invest for each $10,000 that you want in the future at the intersection of the 4-year row and the 5-percent column. In this case, the answer is

Exhibit 2-1. Monthly savings per $10,000 of major expenditure.

Time Horizon (Years)	Monthly Savings Assuming Different Total Returns on Investment				
	4%	5%	6%	7%	8%
1	$818	$814	$811	$807	$803
2	401	397	393	389	386
3	262	258	254	250	247
4	192	$189	185	181	177
5	151	147	143	140	136
10	68	64	61	58	55

Monthly Savings Required

	Example	Your Figures
A. Monthly savings required per $10,000	$189	
Total amount needed in future	$25,000	
Divided by $10,000	÷ $10,000	
B. Multiplier	= 2.50	
C. Monthly savings required (A × B)	$470	

$189 per month, meaning that it takes monthly savings of $189 invested at a 5 percent annual return to accumulate $10,000 in 4 years. If you need $25,000, you must save two and a half times as much. Thus, the example shows that $189 × 2.5 = $470 per month. You can use this approach to establish a financial goal for any major need for cash that you will have within the next 5 years.

Under the 1997 tax law, early withdrawals from IRA accounts

of up to $10,000 may be made without penalty (but not necessarily without paying income taxes) by first-time home buyers. This amount may not help much in California, New York, Alaska, or Hawaii, where housing is very expensive, but it should prove to be a significant benefit in lots of other places. It provides access to a pool of savings, and it enables qualified taxpayers to get the benefit of tax deferrals while they accumulate a down payment on their first house.

MEET COLLEGE COSTS

By the time your new baby goes to college in 18 years, the average total cost of a public college is projected to be about $28,700 per year. This cost level assumes a 6 percent annual increase from the 1997–1998 average cost level of $10,069 per year. According to the College Board, in the 1997–1998 school year, tuition and fees increased by 5 percent for the fifth year in a row. For planning purposes, it is better to project higher costs and save enough to pay them than to fall short if actual costs grow faster than assumed inflation levels. Unfortunately, the inflation rates for college costs are moving targets. Keep track of how fast college costs are rising to be sure that you are saving enough to do the job. The formula for determining future college costs is:

Future college costs = Today's costs × (1 + inflation rate)^{years}.

To make this and other calculations easier, turn to the inflation and growth factors contained in Table A-1 and the monthly savings factors in Table A-2 of the compound interest tables in Appendix A. Restate and solve the above formula, assuming a 6 percent inflation rate for 18 years, as follows:

Future college costs = Today's costs × inflation factor
= $10,069 × 2.85 (6%/18 years)
= $28,700.

A child starting eighth grade today will be ready for college in just 5 years. At that time, you will need an average of $54,000 to pay for 4 years at a public college without any financial assistance. If you have not already started a college fund, you will need to save $730 per month and invest it at an after-tax return of 8 percent in order to accumulate the required amount. (See Exhibit 2-2.) If this dilemma applies to you, you've got lots of work to do to learn about college costs and how to pay for them.

Sending your child to a private college or university could well cost $61,200 per year 18 years from now. In that case, you will need $244,800 at the start of the student's freshman year to pay for tuition and other expenses for 4 years. To accumulate those funds without any help from other sources, you will need to save $510 per month starting while your child is still in diapers.

Once you have a reasonable estimate of what college will cost, you can calculate how much to save and invest by using the following formula (the monthly savings factor comes from Table A-2):

$$
\begin{aligned}
\text{Monthly savings} &= \text{Total future college costs} \times \text{savings factor} \\
&= \$244{,}800 \times 0.00208 \ (8\%/18 \text{ years}) \\
&= \$510.
\end{aligned}
$$

Can you believe it? I'm saying you should already be saving and investing to pay for college, and your child may not even be able to walk yet. And this burden hits you when you probably think you can least afford it. But there is never a good time to start saving, so that's exactly when you should start. Get into the habit *now*. After love and all kinds of support, the best gift for any child is a good education.

USE FEDERAL TAX BREAKS

The passage of the 1997 tax act has made paying for a college education a lot easier—*and* a lot more difficult to understand. How to pay for college has become a complex subject. Eligible taxpayers should take advantage of various federal government benefits contained in the new tax law to help more families pay for their chil-

Exhibit 2-2. Future college costs and monthly savings requirements.

Public College Cost for a Child Starting Eighth Grade

$10,069	Total undergraduate cost today[a]
5.0	Total horizon (years before child enters college)
$0	Financial assistance, initial deposit, or current balance in college fund

Growth Rate in Costs	Future Annual Cost	Total Amount Needed	Monthly Savings Assuming Different Total Returns on Investment			
			6%	8%	10%	12%
2%	$11,100	$44,400	$640	$600	$570	$540
4%	12,300	49,200	710	670	640	600
6%	13,500	54,000	770	$730	700	660
8%	14,800	59,200	850	810	760	720
10%	16,200	64,800	930	880	840	790

Private College Cost for a Newborn Child

$21,424	Total undergraduate cost today[a]
18.0	Time horizon (years before child enters college)
$0	Financial assistance, initial deposit, or current balance in college fund

Growth Rate in Costs	Future Annual Cost	Total Amount Needed	Monthly Savings Assuming Different Total Returns on Investment			
			6%	8%	10%	12%
2%	$30,600	$122,400	$320	$250	$200	$160
4%	43,400	173,600	450	360	290	230
6%	61,200	244,800	630	$510	410	320
8%	85,600	342,400	880	710	570	450
10%	119,100	476,400	1,230	990	790	630

[a]1997–1998 average total costs, including tuition and fees, books and supplies, room and board, transportation, and personal expenses. Source: The College Board.

dren's college education. If your annual income is more than $150,000 for couples or $95,000 for single taxpayers, you can forget about these tax benefits. For those with lower incomes, there are a variety of tax breaks that will help you pay for college.

• *Take advantage of tax credits.* At their current income level, the Smiths are eligible for tax credits totaling $7,000 for the four years their son is at college. Under the Hope Scholarship Credit, they are entitled to a credit of up to $1,500 per year for the cost of tuition and fees (but not for room and board or books) during the first 2 years of college. For subsequent years, the Lifetime Learning Credit will provide up to $1,000 per year until 2003, when its annual limit increases to $2,000. Both credits phase out for joint taxpayers whose adjusted gross income (AGI) is between $80,000 and $100,000. These AGI levels will be indexed for inflation after 2001. If you meet the earnings eligibility requirements, you should take advantage of these tax credits too.

• *Contribute to an Education IRA.* The Smith family can benefit by making a contribution of up to $500 per year ($41.66 per month) to the new Education IRA, which is really an educational savings account rather than a retirement account. When contributions are made for a child age 17 or younger, they are not tax deductible, but interest, dividends, and capital gains accumulate tax free. With an 8 percent annual return, the Smiths can accumulate $7,200 in an Education IRA over the next 10 years before Chris's eighteenth birthday. At that rate, the maximum amount anyone could accumulate over 18 years is $20,000:

$$
\begin{aligned}
\text{Future Education IRA} &= \text{Monthly contribution} \times \text{FV of \$1.00 per month} \\
&= \$41.66 \times 480.09 \ (8\%/18 \text{ years}) \\
&= \$20,000.
\end{aligned}
$$

There are no tax consequences when the funds in an Education IRA are distributed and used to pay for "qualified higher education expenses" (e.g., tuition, fees, books, supplies, equipment, room, and board) for a student between 18 and 30 years old. However, distributions are not tax free if they are made in the same year that one of the tuition tax credits is claimed. The contribution limit is phased out for joint taxpayers with AGI above $150,000. This modified AGI level will be indexed for inflation after 2002.

• *Invest the Child Tax Credit.* If you are eligible for the new Child Tax Credit, the federal government will actually *give* you the money you need to contribute to an Education IRA. Here's how that works. Joint taxpayers with an AGI of $110,000 or less are entitled to a tax credit of $400 in 1998 and $500 in 1999 and thereafter for each child under the age of 17. The qualifying AGI levels will not be indexed for inflation.

Rather than spending this tax savings, you should contribute it, plus an extra $100 for 1998, to an Education IRA. If you do so, the net effect is that the federal government gives you almost all the money to make the contribution and then exempts the earnings on it from taxation. As a practical matter, the government is providing nearly the full value of the Education IRA to each taxpayer who takes advantage of the opportunity. Be sure to take advantage of it if you are eligible.

• *Make penalty-free IRA withdrawals.* The Smiths have each contributed to a traditional IRA in the past, and each will be eligible to make contributions of $2,000 per year to the new *Roth IRA* in the future. This new IRA enables them to accumulate the earnings on their investments entirely tax free. They can also make penalty-free and tax-free withdrawals from a Roth IRA by limiting their withdrawals to the total amount of their contributions. For example, the Smiths may contribute $40,000 over 10 years to a Roth IRA (2 Smiths × $2,000 × 10 years). They can then withdraw the entire $40,000 to pay for college expenses. Thus, all contributions to a Roth IRA should be withdrawn before any penalty-free but taxable withdrawals are made from traditional IRA accounts or from the earnings retained in a Roth IRA. As a practical matter, by using these two IRA accounts plus the new Education IRA, the Smiths can stop worrying about paying taxes on the earnings in their college fund.

• *Deduct interest on education loans.* Finally, joint taxpayers with AGI of $60,000 or less may deduct up to $1,000 in interest on education loans during the first five years that interest payments are required. The maximum allowable deduction is $1,000 in 1998.

It increases by $500 per year until it reaches $2,500 in 2001. This interest deduction helps reduce the cost of borrowing to meet educational expenses. The qualifying AGI levels will be indexed for inflation after 2002.

Another way to deduct interest on a loan to meet education expenses is to borrow against the equity in your home. Since mortgage interest is also tax deductible, you can get a deduction in this way too. If your income level rules out deductibility on a standard student loan, a home equity loan will probably have the best terms and lowest after-tax cost.

When all these benefits are added up, the government will end up paying a significant portion of the college expenses of many students, a terrific deal for parents. The current estimate for Chris Smith's college costs for 4 years at a public college, shown in Exhibit 2-3, is $72,000. After tapping government tax credits that provide a total of $7,000, Bill and Bonnie Smith must accumulate $65,000 over the next 10 years. Fortunately, Chris's grandparents have set aside $4,000 in one of their mutual fund accounts, and they will pay any income taxes that are due on its earnings. That $4,000 is expected to grow by 8 percent annually, reaching $8,600 by the time Chris starts his freshman year. His parents need additional funds of $56,400 ($65,000 − $8,600) by then. To meet that need, they must save and invest $425 per month ($5,100 per year) at an average 8 percent return. This amount represents 7.1 percent of the Smith's combined salaries, a significant commitment. The Smiths plan to contribute the $42 per month to an Education IRA, a total of $333 per month to their two Roth IRAs, and the remaining $50 they need to a taxable account. You too need to take all these federal tax benefits into account when you plan how much you must save and invest for your children's education.

You can use the exhibit to estimate the amount you must invest to accumulate your own college fund. In addition, Fidelity Investments has a program, the College Cost Calculator, that you can use to determine how much you should save. It is available by mail and may be found on America Online and the Internet. Schwab also has an excellent program, The Schwab College Saver Program, available on its Web site.

Exhibit 2-3. How much to save for your college fund.

		Smith Family	Your Figures
Number of years until college		10	
Annual cost of college in today's dollars		$10,069	
Times: Inflation factor (Table A-1) (6%/10 years)	×	1.79	
A. Annual cost in future dollars	=	$18,000	
Times: Number of years at college	×	4	
B. Total amount needed at start of college	=	($72,000)	( )
C. Less: Amounts provided by other sources			
Hope Scholarship Credits (2 × $1,500): 1st 2 years		$3,000	
Lifelong Learning Credits (2 × $2,000): 2nd 2 years		4,000	
Gifts from others paid directly to college (no gift tax)		0	
Financial aid: Grants or loans		0	
Total from other sources		7,000	
D. Net amount required (B − C)		($65,000)	( )
Held in grandparents' account ↘			
Current college fund		$4,000	
Times: Growth factor (Table A-1) (8%/10 years)	×	2.16	
E. Future value of current college fund	=	$8,600	
F. Additional amount required (D − E)		($56,400)	( )
G. Withdrawals from parents' IRA accounts			
Education IRA ($500/year @ 8% for 10 years)		$7,200	
Roth IRAs: Tax-free withdrawals ($2,000 × 2 for 10 years)		40,000	
Traditional IRAs: Taxable withdrawals (net of taxes)		0	
Total from parents' IRAs		$47,200	
H. Remaining shortfall (future dollars) (F − G)		($9,200)	( )
Times: Monthly savings factor (Table A-2)	×	0.00547	
(8%/10 years) ↗			
Monthly savings to close shortfall	=	50	
Plus: Contributions to Education IRA ($500/year ÷ 12)	+	42	
Plus: Contributions to Roth IRAs ($2,000/year × 2 ÷ 12)	+	333	
Total monthly savings required	=	($425)	( )
Monthly savings as a % of monthly income		(7.1%)	( )

• *Watch Eligibility Phase-Out Levels.* As you plan, you must pay attention to one of the most confusing aspects of the 1997 tax breaks for higher education: the income eligibility levels. The tax benefits are available only to taxpayers below certain income levels. Accordingly, they start to phase out at a specified level of AGI and are completely eliminated when income reaches a higher level. Unfortunately for those who favor a simpler tax code, these phase-out ranges are different for different benefits. Here are the eligibility phase-out levels for single and joint taxpayers for each of the college-related benefits included in the new tax law:

College-Related Tax Benefit	1998 Benefit Phase-Out Levels in AGI		
	Single	Joint	Indexing
Education IRA	$95,000–$110,000	$150,000–$160,000	After 2002
Roth IRA	$95,000–$110,000	$150,000–$160,000	None
Child Tax Credit	$75,000–$ 85,000	$110,000–$120,000	None
Hope Scholarship Credit	$40,000–$ 50,000	$ 80,000–$100,000	After 2001
Lifelong Learning Credit	$40,000–$ 50,000	$ 80,000–$100,000	After 2001
Deductible loan interest	$40,000–$ 50,000	$ 60,000–$ 75,000	After 2002
Traditional IRA	$30,000–$ 40,000	$ 50,000–$ 60,000	Until 2005 (single taxpayers)/2007 (joint taxpayers)

Obviously, your income level could make you eligible for some benefits but not for others. To add to the confusion, some of the phase-out ranges will be indexed for inflation starting at different times in the future. Since both your income and the phase-out levels will probably be changing in the future, you should keep up-to-date on which benefits apply to you.

KEEP THE MONEY IN YOUR NAME

One of the issues that many parents face is whether they should hold funds earmarked for their children's education in their own names or put it in a custodial account in the child's name. Custodial accounts include those that come under the Uniform Gift to Minors Act (UGMA) or the Uniform Transfers to Minors Act (UTMA), depending on the state where you live. In both cases, the transfer of money or other assets is irrevocable. The choice between using a custodial account and maintaining the funds in a brokerage account in your name involves a trade-off between control and eligibility for financial aid on the one hand and tax savings on the other.

- *Maintain control and flexibility.* When the child reaches age 18 or 21, depending on the state, the child has the right to take and spend the money on whatever he or she wants—including a hot new motorcycle or a trip around the world. In that case, all the money that you save and invest may not produce the result you want. If you are concerned about how your child might use the money, maintain control over the college fund so that it can be spent only in ways that you approve. You can always shift funds into a custodial account in your child's name, but once it is in the child's name, you can't shift it back. For control and flexibility, keep the money in your name.

- *Improve chances for financial aid.* The rules regarding college financial aid also favor keeping the college fund in your name. According to financial aid formulas, 35 percent of a student's assets are assumed to be available to pay college expenses, but only 5.6 percent of parents' assets, excluding retirement accounts and principal residence, are counted. Thus, keeping assets in the parents' name is the clear winner. Too many people assume incorrectly that they are too wealthy to qualify for financial aid. If you expect, need, or want any financial aid or if you just want to keep your options open, keep the college fund in your name.

- *Consider tax implications.* Just to make the choice more difficult, tax considerations argue for using a custodial account in your child's name. In that case, any taxable income it earns may be subject to the so-called kiddie tax. If the child is under age 14 and has only investment income, the kiddie tax applies. For 1998, the first $700 of investment income is free from tax, and the second $700 is taxed at 15 percent. Therefore, the total federal tax on the first $1,400 is $105. This $1,400 in income could be generated by $14,000 in investments earning 10 percent per year, or $28,000 earning 5 percent, and numerous other combinations of investment balances and earnings rates.

Any income above $1,400 is taxed at the parents' top marginal rate—the rate that would apply if the assets were held in the parents' name. The federal tax savings from application of the kiddie tax rather than the parents' top marginal rate could be as much as $450 per year ($1,400 × 39.6% − $105). The annual savings is $287 for taxpayers in the 28 percent bracket. If invested at 8 percent, these savings could add up to more than $4,000 over a 14-year period. Once the child becomes 14, all income is taxed at the child's rate as an individual taxpayer, presumably a lower rate than the parents' rate. As a result, try not to sell assets that trigger the capital gains tax until the child reaches 14. If you are not concerned about keeping the assets under your control and you are sure that financial aid is not in your plans, put the money in your child's name. Otherwise, forgo the tax savings and keep it in yours.

ADJUST ASSET MIX AS COLLEGE APPROACHES

Since they have a 10-year time horizon before college, the Smiths should invest the bulk of their college fund in equity mutual funds in the next few years while they have plenty of time to overcome the impact of any market decline. Over time, they should gradually shift their investment mix toward fixed income investments, investing almost entirely in short-term bond and money market funds within a few years of when their first tuition payment is due. By following this approach, they will minimize the risk of a reduction in their college fund due to a market decline or changes in interest rates. They can be sure they will have the money they need for Chris's college expenses when the time comes.

ENSURE A COMFORTABLE RETIREMENT

Two facts about retirement should be clear. First, the potential costs of retirement are awesome. Second, most of us have to fund a major portion of our retirement income ourselves.

Social security benefits are likely to grow at a reduced rate in order to preserve the viability of the system. In the private sector, many companies are putting increased emphasis on retirement plans that require employee contributions. The net result is that social security and company pension plans will not provide us the income we require to maintain the same standard of living that we have enjoyed during our working years.

To determine what you must do to enjoy a financially comfortable retirement, you should answer these questions, in this order:

- When do you want to retire from the occupation that provides your principal source of income?
- How much income will you need to maintain your standard of living during retirement?
- How large should your investment portfolio be to provide the required retirement income?
- How much do you need to invest, and at what rate of return, in order to build the required portfolio?

By taking into account what you already know and making some assumptions about other amounts, time horizons, and interest rates, you can quantify your retirement needs.

WHEN TO RETIRE?

By definition, "to retire" is to stop working at your present job and start doing something else with your life. Naturally, retirement may mean different things to different people—golf, travel, more time with your family, a hobby, volunteer work, or another vocation that you have always wanted to pursue. Whatever activities you choose for your retirement years, early planning and faithful implementation of your plans should make them possible.

When you retire, you shift from an *accumulation phase*, in which you save and invest to build your portfolio, to a *withdrawal phase*, when you continue to manage your investment portfolio but withdraw funds to support yourself rather than contributing to your portfolio through savings. Of course, your portfolio may still continue to grow if it earns more than you require for living expenses, a likely outcome for at least several years.

There is nothing magical about when to retire. You can retire whenever you want—*if* you can afford it. From a financial perspective, the most important result of retirement is that when you leave your job, your primary source of income will be eliminated. Thus, you can afford to retire only when you have sufficient income from other sources to support yourself and those dependent on you for the rest of your life.

The challenge is to develop those other sources of income so that when you can *afford* to retire is the same as when you *want* to retire. It is obvious that the sooner you want to retire, the more you must save and invest. If you want to retire early, you may also have to take on a higher level of risk in order to achieve the returns that you need.

There are also a few government- or employer-mandated dates that may influence your choice of retirement age. Depending on your age, full social security retirement benefits currently start at ages 65 to 67. At age 62 you can start receiving reduced social security payments. With few exceptions, withdrawals from your IRA, 401(k), or Keogh plans may not be made without a penalty until age 59$^1/_2$. Another consideration is when your company's pension plan, if it has one, permits you to take early or regular retirement and the amount of your benefit in each case.

The Smiths want to retire in 20 years when Bill reaches age 65 and Bonnie becomes 62. They also plan for 25 years of retirement, until Bill becomes 90. With that assumption, they can be comfortable that they will not outlive their money, a grim situation.

You should specify the age at which you want to retire and assume that you will also live to be 90 years old. If you are unsure what age to choose, pick 65 and develop your plan with that assumption in mind. After you see the results, you may change the assumption and see how the change affects how much you must save and invest. Such calculations may also help you assess whether you will be able to retire when you want or whether you must change one or more of the variables in your plan.

How Much Income?

As shown in Exhibit 2-4, the Smiths will need monthly income of $10,500 starting at their retirement date. Using the inflation and growth factors, they calculate that they can expect or want to rely on only $3,100 per month from other sources. To be conservative, they use a 4 percent inflation rate in their calculations because it is

Exhibit 2-4. Monthly retirement income required from an investment portfolio.

	Smith Family	Your Figures
Current gross monthly income	$6,000	_____
Times: Retirement factor (70–90%) ×	80%	_____
Monthly retirement income in today's dollars =	$4,800	_____
Times: Inflation factor (Table A-1) ×	2.19	_____
A. Monthly retirement income needed =	($10,500)	◯
(starting at retirement date, in future dollars)		
	4% inflation for 20 years	
Monthly retirement income from other sources	$1,400	_____
(social security, pension, work, home equity)		
Times: Inflation factor (Table A-1) ×	2.19	
B. Monthly income provided by other sources =	($3,100)	◯
(starting at retirement date, in future dollars)		
C. Income from investment portfolio (A − B)	($7,400)	◯
(carry over to Exhibit 2-6)		

slightly higher than the average for recent years. Thus, their investment portfolio must produce $7,400 per month in future dollars. These figures make clear the challenge they face to ensure a comfortable retirement. The income they must generate from their investment portfolio is more than their current salaries. You may face the same challenge.

You should determine how much retirement income you will need or want to have. A rule of thumb for this *retirement factor* is that it will take between 70 and 90 percent of your preretirement income to maintain the same standard of living during retirement. The best way to pin down your needs is to prepare a postretirement budget in today's dollars. List your current monthly expenses and identify how much you need of each expense item if you retired today. Be sure to take into account work-related expenses, including social security and Medicare taxes, that you will no longer have after retirement.

If you don't want to prepare a detailed budget, use 80 percent of your gross monthly income as an initial estimate of the monthly retirement income you will need. You can always adjust the percentage or develop a more precise figure if you think a different dollar amount is more appropriate for you.

Then estimate the monthly income that you expect from other sources, such as social security, a company pension, inheritance, postretirement employment, or the equity in your home. To find out your expected social security income, call 1-800-772-1213 and ask for Form SSA-7004, "Request for Earnings and Benefit Estimate Statement." Fill out the form, and mail it to the Social Security Administration (SSA). You will receive your Personal Earnings and Benefit Estimate Statement (PEBES) within a few weeks. It will tell you what your social security retirement benefits will be, expressed in today's dollars. The request form is also available on the SSA Web site on the Internet (http://www.ssa.gov). Once you access the Web site you can (1) print out the form and send it in by mail, (2) file your information electronically and receive your PEBES by mail, or (3) file your information electronically and get your PEBES on-line. My choice is to get the information immediately.

The $500,000 tax exemption for married couples filing jointly ($250,000 for single taxpayers) on gains on the sale of primary residences is a huge benefit for many Americans. As a practical matter, it eliminates any taxes on home sales for all but a very small portion of the population. After all, your house must be worth at least $500,000 in order for you to have a $500,000 gain. As a result of this provision, more people are likely to use the equity in their homes as sources of retirement income in the future.

In addition, the gradual increase in the federal estate tax exemption from $625,000 in 1998 to $1 million in 2006 will result in more money being passed on to heirs and available to fund the heirs' retirement.

You should get as much information as you can about these other potential sources, and then decide which ones and what amounts to rely on in planning your retirement needs. Any of these figures provided by outside sources may be expressed in today's dollars or in future dollars. Be sure you know which time horizon is used and make adjustments as required using the compound interest tables. The formulas for converting present values to future amounts, and vice versa, are:

$$\text{Future value} = \text{Present value} \times \text{growth factor}$$

and

$$\text{Present value} = \text{Future value} \div \text{growth factor.}$$

Finally, determine the income that you must provide for yourself from your own investment portfolio. Providing this level of income is, by definition, one of your major financial goals.

WHEN TO TAKE SOCIAL SECURITY?

Every American eligible to receive social security retirement benefits must decide when to start taking those benefits. If you are close to 60 years old, you should contact the SSA to be sure you understand your options, including the impact of continuing to work while receiving retirement benefits. If retirement is decades away, feel free to skip to the next topic, or read on so that you can provide good advice to your parents.

Full retirement benefits currently start at age 65 for those born in 1937 or earlier and at age 67 for those born in 1960 and later. Those born in between have retirement ages ranging from 65 to 67. You can take early retirement as early as age 62. If you do, your benefits will be reduced based on the number of monthly checks you will receive prior to reaching your full retirement age. If your full retirement age is 65, you may start receiving benefits equal to 80 percent of the full benefit at age 62. Should you take retirement 3 years early or wait until your full retirement date?

The basic rule is that you should take your 80 percent early retirement benefit as long as your earned income level doesn't trigger a significant benefit reduction. The calculations that support this conclusion are shown in Exhibit 2-5. They assume a 4 percent annual cost of living adjustment for benefits and the ability to invest at 8 percent per year. The exhibit shows, for ages 62 and 65, the annual amounts you would receive per $1,000 of full retirement

Exhibit 2-5. When to take social security: Age 62 or 65? (Amounts are per $1,000 of full annual retirement benefit.)

Assumptions		Net Present Value to Age 85	
8.0%	Earnings rate (pretax)		
4.0%	Inflation rate	**$11,915**	If taken at age 62
$1,000	Annual benefit at age 65	**$10,862**	If taken at age 65
$ 800	Annual benefit at age 62		

	Take at Age 62			Take at Age 65			Age 62 Advantage	
Age	Annual Receipt	Cumulative Receipts	Investment Balance	Annual Receipt	Cumulative Receipts	Investment Balance	Cumulative Receipts	Investment Balance
62	$ 800	$ 800	$ 800	$ 0	$ 0	$ 0	$ 800	$ 800
63	832	1,632	1,696	0	0	0	1,632	1,696
64	865	2,497	2,697	0	0	0	2,497	2,697
65	900	3,397	3,813	1,000	1,000	1,000	2,397	2,813
66	936	4,333	5,054	1,040	2,040	2,120	2,293	2,934
67	973	5,306	6,431	1,082	3,122	3,371	2,185	3,060
68	1,012	6,319	7,958	1,125	4,246	4,766	2,072	3,192
69	1,053	7,371	9,647	1,170	5,416	6,317	1,955	3,330
70	1,095	8,466	11,514	1,217	6,633	8,039	1,833	3,475
71	1,139	9,605	13,574	1,265	7,898	9,947	1,707	3,626
72	1,184	10,789	15,844	1,316	9,214	12,059	1,575	3,785
73	1,232	12,021	18,343	1,369	10,583	14,392	1,438	3,950
74	1,281	13,301	21,091	1,423	12,006	16,967	1,295	4,124
75	1,332	14,634	24,110	1,480	13,486	19,805	1,147	4,306
76	1,385	16,019	27,425	1,539	15,026	22,928	993	4,496
77	1,441	17,460	31,059	1,601	16,627	26,364	833	4,695
78	1,498	18,958	35,042	1,665	18,292	30,138	666	4,904
79	1,558	20,516	39,404	1,732	20,024	34,281	493	5,123
80	1,621	22,137	44,177	1,801	21,825	38,824	312	5,353
81	1,685	23,822	49,397	1,873	23,698	43,803	125	5,594
82	1,753	25,575	55,101	1,948	25,645	49,255	−$70	5,846
83	1,823	27,398	61,332	2,026	27,671	55,221	−273	6,111
84	1,896	29,294	68,135	2,107	29,778	61,746	−484	6,389
85	1,972	31,266	75,558	2,191	31,969	68,877	−703	6,681
86	2,051	33,317	83,653	2,279	34,248	76,666	−931	6,987
87	2,133	35,449	92,478	2,370	36,618	85,169	−1,168	7,309
88	2,218	37,667	102,094	2,465	39,083	94,447	−1,415	7,647
89	2,307	39,974	112,568	2,563	41,646	104,566	−1,672	8,002
90	2,399	42,373	123,972	2,666	44,312	115,597	−1,939	8,375

benefit. For each case, it projects cumulative receipts and the total investment balance at the end of each year if all receipts were invested at the assumed earnings rate. Finally, it shows the advantage of taking retirement at age 62 in terms of both cumulative receipts and the investment balance.

If you need the money for living expenses, you should take the early benefit, and spend it wisely. By starting at age 62, your annual benefit will always be less than if you waited until age 65. However, the cumulative amount you will receive will be higher until you reach 82 years old. It takes that long for larger amounts starting at age 65 to overcome the advantage of receiving the money early.

If you do not need the income to live on, and your earnings are less than the amount you can earn without penalty ($9,120 in 1998), you should still take the early retirement benefit. In that case, invest it wisely, and reinvest any interest and dividends. As long as you can earn an attractive rate of return, you will accumulate a larger investment pool than you could by starting at age 65 and maximize the value of your retirement benefit.

Finally, if you are at least 62 but not yet 65, and you are earning more than the allowed limit, your payment will be reduced by $1 for every $2 you earn above the limit. Thus, if you are earning $35,000, your social security benefit would be reduced by $12,940—probably a large part of your potential benefit. In that case, you should not take the early benefit. Even after you reach 65, your benefit will be reduced by $1 for each $3 you earn in excess of an annual limit ($14,500 for 1998). Accordingly, assess the impact of these earnings limits on your total income before deciding to take your social security retirement benefits.

WHAT SIZE OF RETIREMENT FUND?

It takes a fund of $535,000, invested at 8 percent, to provide annual income of $50,000 for 25 years of retirement, with nothing left after the twenty-fifth year. This equal annual payment is an annuity. Like a typical mortgage payment, it comprises both investment income and a portion of the principal. At the end of the specified time period, the principal is depleted. Nothing is left. This approach is used throughout the book. Alternatively, if you want to preserve the principal for your heirs and live off earnings only, a larger retirement fund (in this case, an endowment of $625,000) will be required.

Unfortunately, surveys show that many Americans do not grasp how much capital they will need to retire at even half their current income levels. A nest egg of $100,000, seemingly a lot of money, will provide annuity income of only $9,400 per year for 25 years, hardly enough to live on. In 1994, $9,400 was only slightly more than the official poverty level for a two-person family age 65 and older.

You can use the information in Exhibit 2-6 to determine how large your retirement fund must be. It takes $129,600, invested at 8 percent, to provide monthly income of $1,000 for 25 years. This amount, times a multiplier based on the monthly income require- ment that you previously determined, equals your target retire- ment fund. Your investment portfolio must grow to this amount by the time you retire. The worst thing you can do is to outlive your money, and your life expectancy is probably much longer than you think. To be safe, the exhibit assumes that you will live to be 90 years old.

The Smiths need an investment portfolio of $959,000 in future dollars to provide the monthly income that they require. Unbeliev- able! Nearly a million dollars! Fortunately, their current portfolio of $120,000 is expected to grow to $559,000 by the time they retire. Thus, their savings and investment activities must produce addi- tional funds of $400,000 during the next 20 years. These figures seem huge, but they are realistic for a couple with the Smiths' time horizon, financial situation, and goals.

HOW MUCH TO SAVE?

The best way to accumulate wealth, other than inheriting it, is to put away as much as you can each month. Unfortunately, Depart- ment of Commerce figures show that personal savings declined from 5.1 percent of personal income in 1980 to 3.6 percent in 1994. This level of savings is not enough if you want a comfortable retire- ment.

Exhibit 2-6. Investment portfolio required to produce monthly income of $1,000.

Retirement Age	Years of Retirement to Age 90	Invesment Portfolio Assuming Different Total Returns on Investment			
		6%	8%	10%	12%
80	10	$ 90,100	$ 82,400	$ 75,700	$ 69,700
75	15	118,500	104,600	93,100	83,300
70	20	139,600	119,600	103,600	90,800
65	25	155,200	$129,600	110,000	94,900
60	30	166,800	136,300	114,000	97,200
55	35	175,400	140,800	116,300	98,500
50	40	181,700	143,800	117,800	99,200

Total and Additional Portfolio Required

		Smith Family	Your Figures
A. Portfolio per $1,000 of monthly income		$129,600	
Monthly income needed (see Exhibit 2-4)		$7,400	
Divided by $1,000	÷	$1,000	
B. Multiplier	=	7.4	
C. Total investment portfolio required (A × B)	=	$959,000	
(at retirement date, in future dollars)			
Current investment portfolio (see Exhibit 1-1)		$120,000	
Times: Growth factor (Table A-1)	×	4.66	
D. Future value of current investment portfolio	=	$559,000	
(at retirement date, in future dollars)			
E. Additional funds required (C − D)	=	$400,000	
(at retirement date, in future dollars)			
			(carry over to Exhibit 2-9)

You should invest at least 13 percent of your monthly gross income, including contributions that you make to an IRA, 401(k), or Keogh plan *and* any matching contributions that your employer makes to your 401(k) account for your benefit. If you can afford it, make the entire 13 percent investment yourself, and treat your employer's contribution as an extra benefit. Better yet, if your employer permits you to contribute more than 13 percent, do everything you can to make that maximum contribution. To put it in perspective, employers deduct 7.65 percent for social security and medicare on the first $68,400 of 1998 gross income. By saving a constant percentage of your income, the amount you save will increase as your income grows. The savings should not be painful, and you will accumulate a much larger nest egg over time.

Why save and invest 13 percent of your salary? I call it the "Magic 13 Percent" because if you maintain that practice over a 40-year working life (from ages 25 to 65), you will be able to retire and live comfortably for the rest of your life. The investment portfolio produced by this rate of saving and investing is enough to provide you with a 25-year annuity equal to 108 percent of your final working salary. This benefit for each $10,000 of your current salary is shown by the figures in Exhibit 2-7. In this example, the amount stays constant each year in the future; it does not increase with inflation.

Columns 5 and 6 of Exhibit 2-7 track your progress toward accumulating the capital needed to fund your retirement. For each year, they show (1) the immediate annuity that each year-end portfolio would produce from then to age 90 and (2) the portion of your current salary represented by that annuity. Column 7 shows the size of the portfolio relative to your salary in each year.

At an 8 percent return, to produce a 25-year annuity equal to your final salary before retirement requires a portfolio of over 12 times that salary. Alternatively, saving 13 percent of your salary each year will enable you to build an investment portfolio that, invested at 8 percent, will provide income equal to 80 percent of your final salary during your first year of retirement and then keep up with yearly inflation of 4 percent for the next 25 years of retirement—until age 90. If you start your investment program later or expect a longer retirement period or a higher rate of inflation, you will need to save a higher percentage of your earned income. If

Exhibit 2-7. The Magic 13 percent savings rate.

Assumptions

A.	$10,000	**Current salary**
B.	4.0%	**Salary increase and inflation rate**
C.	8.0%	**Investment rate of return**
D.	13.0%	**Percent of salary saved and invested**

Year	(1) Annual Salary	(2) Yearly Savings	(3) Investment Income	(4) Year-End Portfolio	(5) Annuity to Age 90	(6) Annuity % of Salary	(7) Portfolio ÷ Salary
Calculation:	(A × 1 + B)	(1 + D)	(C × (4 + 2/2))	(4 + 2 + 3)	(At C%)	(5 ÷ 1)	(4 ÷ 1)
1	$10,000	$1,300	$ 50	$ 1,350	$ 100	1%	0.1
5	11,600	1,510	570	8,500	640	6	0.7
10	14,100	1,830	1,620	22,810	1,710	12	1.6
15	17,200	2,240	3,330	46,070	3,490	20	2.7
20	20,900	2,720	6,040	82,960	6,340	30	4.0
25	25,400	3,300	10,280	140,430	10,900	43	5.5
30	30,900	4,020	16,810	228,900	18,190	59	7.4
35	37,500	4,870	26,760	363,730	29,920	80	9.7
40	45,700	5,940	41,840	567,780	49,250	108%	12.4

you can consistently earn a higher rate of return, you can build a retirement fund with smaller annual contributions.

The figures in Exhibit 2-8 provide further perspective on the importance of your savings rate and the investment rate of return. They illustrate the logical conclusion that if you save more and/or invest to earn higher rates of return, you will enjoy a higher level of retirement income. Specifically, the exhibit shows the size of the annuity that your investment portfolio could produce, expressed as a percentage of your final salary before retirement, at different rates of savings and return on investment over a 40-year period. Thus, you can accumulate enough money to obtain about the same 25-year annuity if you save 17 percent of your salary and invest it at 7 percent, 9 percent of your salary at 9 percent, 5 percent of your salary at 11 percent, and so forth.

It takes a monthly investment of only $170, invested at 8 per-

Exhibit 2-8. Potential 25-year annuities as a percentage of final salary (4% inflation, 40-year time horizon).

Percentage of Salary Saved	Investment Rate of Return (annual)					
	7%	8%	9%	10%	11%	12%
	Potential 25-Year Annuities as a Percentage of Final Salary					
20%	122%	166%	226%	308%	422%	579%
19	116	158	215	293	401	550
18	110	149	203	278	380	521
17	(104%)	141	192	262	359	492
16	98	133	181	247	338	463
15	92	124	169	231	316	434
14	86	116	158	216	295	405
Magic 13%	80	(108%)	147	200	274	376
12	73	99	135	185	253	348
11	67	91	124	170	232	319
10	61	83	113	154	211	290
9	55	75	(102%)	139	190	261
8	49	66	90	123	169	232
7	43	58	79	(108%)	148	203
6	37	50	68	93	127	174
5	30	41	56	77	(105%)	144

cent, to produce a retirement fund of $100,000 in 20 years (see Exhibit 2-9). To determine the monthly investment you will need for your retirement fund, first identify the monthly investment required to produce a retirement fund of $100,000 based on your estimated years to retirement and rate of return. Then use the worksheet at the bottom of the exhibit to complete your calculations. For the Smiths, the monthly investment is $680, which represents 11.3 percent of their monthly income.

Exhibit 2-9. Monthly investment required to produce a portfolio of $100,000.

Current Age	Years to Retirement at Age 65	Monthly Investment Assuming Different Total Return on Investment			
		6%	8%	10%	12%
60	5	$1,430	$1,360	$1,290	$1,220
55	10	610	550	490	430
50	15	340	290	240	200
45	20	220	$170	130	100
40	25	140	110	80	50
35	30	100	70	40	30
30	35	70	40	30	20
25	40	50	30	20	10

Monthly Investment Required

	Smith Family	Your Figures
A. Monthly investment required per $100,000	$170	
Additional funds required (Exhibit 2-6)	$400,000	
Divided by $100,000	÷ $100,000	
B. Multiplier	= 4.00	
C. Monthly investment for retirement fund (A × B)	= $680	
Total investment % of monthly income	11.3%	
D. Employer 401(k) matching contributions	$180	
(must be maximum contribution)		
Employer contribution % of income (Exhibit 1-1)	3.0%	
(50% of 6% of salary = 3% of salary)		
E. Employee 401(k) contributions (C−D)	$500	
(must not exceed 1998 maximum of $10,000 or $833 per month)		
Employee contribution % of monthly income	8.3%	
(must be at least 6% to qualify for maximum employer contribution)		

Fortunately, the Smiths' current employers provide $180 per month, or 3 percent of their monthly income, through matching provisions of their 401(k) plans. The employers contribute 50 cents for each dollar contributed by the Smiths, up to a maximum of 6 percent of their salaries. The Smiths make sure that they qualify for the maximum employer contribution. As a result, the Smiths themselves must contribute only $500 per month, or 8.3 percent of their income, to their tax-deferred retirement accounts.

They can save and invest less than the Magic 13 Percent because they already have a portfolio that will provide a major part of their future financial needs. Nevertheless, they should strive to increase their 401(k) contributions to the maximum permitted levels so they can take full advantage of the benefits of tax deferrals. By doing so, they may be able to retire earlier or with a higher level of retirement income. Their maximum levels are the lesser of 15 percent of salary, a limit set by their employers, and the dollar limit permitted by the tax laws: $10,000 for each person in 1998. They are currently forgoing additional contributions of $333 per month, which represents 5.6 percent of their salaries. At the very least, they should continue to invest the same portion of their incomes every month. If they follow this program, with an annual checkup and adjustment if needed to stay on track, they will achieve their financial goals.

WHAT IF YOU CAN'T SAVE ENOUGH?

What if you can't possibly save the amounts indicated by your calculations? Are you doomed to poverty in your old age? No, but you have just received one of the major benefits of personal financial planning: a heavy dose of realism. What should you do? Start by checking your figures to make sure they are right and that you believe them. If they are correct, it is important to recognize that you've got a problem. It is a problem that you can do something about, but it isn't usually a quick-fix solution.

Simply stated, you are spending too much and not saving enough. Determine the amount of your savings shortfall. Is it $50 per month or $500 per month? To close the gap, you need to increase your income or reduce your spending, or both—and it is likely to take a while to accomplish. For example, it could mean a new job, a less expensive home, a cheaper car, or less dining out. As a first step, find something you can cut out of your monthly budget so that you can save more. See if you can increase your 401(k) contribution by a comparable amount. When you pay your bills each month, make a practice of contributing to your investment program first.

Concentrate your efforts over the next year on ways to increase your income and cut your costs. Do not be discouraged. Chances are that you have lots of time to get back on track. If you cannot find a way to increase your income or reduce your costs over the next few years, you will have to adopt a more realistic goal for your retirement. Before you take that step, however, do everything in your power to spend less and save more. It's simple to say and hard to do. Try harder.

PROVIDE FOR HEIRS

Some people want to leave a large estate to their heirs. Others would like to do that but realistically will be unable to achieve that goal. Still others want to spend every last dollar while they're alive to enjoy it. They figure it's up to the heirs to take care of themselves. There is no correct position on providing for heirs. It's a matter of personal philosophy and choice.

If, upon your death, you want to provide for your children, grandchildren, other people, or a favorite charity, there are three ways that you can accomplish that goal: (1) name whomever you want to receive your estate in your will or revocable trust; (2) during your lifetime, establish a separate heirs' fund to ensure that a specific amount will pass to your heirs at a designated time; and (3) buy life insurance and name your chosen heirs as beneficiaries.

YOUR ESTATE

When you die, your remaining net worth will go to your heirs in accordance with the terms of your will or of any trusts you create.

If you die before the age 90 planning horizon for your retirement fund, they will get the remaining principal from that fund. You may also plan to have some wealth left over past age 90. If your retirement portfolio is large enough so that you can live off its income without touching the principal, or at least without reducing it below the amount you want your heirs to inherit, this approach will provide an estate for your heirs.

This approach is the easiest. It requires no additional savings and no investment decisions. However, the amount that your heirs will receive, if any, is uncertain. It's a function of the size of your estate, the level of your living expenses, and your age when you die. It could be a lot of money, or it could be little or none. If you want more certainty regarding how much your heirs will receive, use one of the other two approaches.

AN HEIRS' FUND

You may make periodic contributions to a separate fund for the benefit of your heirs. In its simplest form, this fund could be a separate account in your name that you informally tag for your heirs. At the other extreme, it could be in one or more irrevocable trusts. If the idea of an heirs' fund appeals to you, be sure to discuss it with your tax adviser and a lawyer so that you understand the income tax, gift tax, estate tax, and other consequences before you act.

To decide how much to contribute, establish a monthly goal in today's dollars and project it into the future to the year in which you want your heirs to receive it. Then convert the future monthly amount into a lump sum. Finally, determine how much you must save and invest each month, at an 8 percent annual return, to accumulate the future lump sum. These calculations are illustrated in Exhibit 2-10. They show that it will take a current monthly contribution of $240, or 4 percent of the Smiths' monthly income, to generate an heirs' fund in 20 years that is large enough to provide an annuity of $500 in today's dollars for the following 25 years.

The mechanics of a fund for heirs are no different from one earmarked for a major expenditure, college expenses, or retirement. A shortcut is simply to pick a lump-sum amount that you

Exhibit 2-10. Monthly savings and investment required for an heirs' fund.

		Example	Your Figures
Target monthly income in today's dollars		$500	
Times: Inflation factor (Table A-1) (4%/20 years)	×	2.19	
A. Target monthly income in future dollars	=	$1,100	
Divided by $1,000	÷	$1,000	
Multiplier	=	1.10	
Portfolio per $1,000 of monthly income	×	$129,600	
(from Exhibit 2-6—8% annual return for 25 years)			
B. Target heirs' fund in future dollars	=	$143,000	
(in 20 years, rounded to nearest thousand)			
Divided by $100,000	÷	$100,000	
Multiplier	=	1.43	
Monthly investment required per $100,000	×	$170	
(from Exhibit 2-9—8% annual return for 20 years)			
C. Monthly investment in heirs' fund	=	$240	
Monthly investment % of monthly income		4.0%	

would like to provide at a specific time in the future and then figure out how much you must save each month to accumulate that amount. Naturally you should satisfy yourself that you can afford it.

LIFE INSURANCE

Life insurance is the best way to create an instant estate. It is especially helpful to a family with young children whose parents have launched their savings and investment program but currently have accumulated only a fraction of their needs. Life insurance can fill the gap between their needs and their current portfolio. If the parents should die, the children's future will be financially secure.

• *How much coverage?* For most people, life insurance is likely to be the primary means of providing for minor children when the principal wage earners are no longer around to do that job. Using an 8 percent investment rate and assuming no invasion of principal, a life insurance policy that will take the place of a wage earner will need to be 12.5 times the lost income it must make up. Thus, the Smith family should think in terms of having life insurance of $525,000 on Bill's life and $375,000 on Bonnie's life. These amounts represent the maximum, or most conservative, amount of coverage that the Smiths need. They can reduce or terminate their coverage as their investment portfolio's goals are achieved or maintain the coverage as part of a plan to provide additional wealth to their heirs.

• *What type of policy?* The right choice is to buy a term life policy from a quality company. Avoid whole life policies, universal life policies, and anything that pays an agent's commission or has a buildup of cash surrender value—the amount you can get by cashing in the policy. You want to buy pure insurance coverage rather than a policy that has both an insurance and an investment feature. Such investment features typically underperform what you can earn in your investment portfolio. The specific type of policy could be annual renewable term (also called yearly renewable term, YRT), in which the premium increases each year, or 10-, 15-, or 20-year level premium, in which the premium is guaranteed to be constant for the life of the policy. Naturally, level premiums are higher for policies with longer time horizons (i.e., the annual premium for a 10-year term policy is higher than the premium for a 5-year term). They are also higher than the premiums in the early years of a YRT. Your choice should depend on the specifics of the contracts you are offered. Be sure to buy the optional *waiver of premium benefit,* which will pay the premium for you if you should ever become disabled and unable to make the premium payments.

• *What does it cost?* Obviously life insurance policies are cheaper when you are young and more expensive as you age. Be sure to shop aggressively for a term life policy because premiums vary a lot among companies. Naturally, your medical history is important, and rates for smokers are much, much higher than for nonsmokers. Annual premiums for term life policies offered by

Exhibit 2-11. Annual life insurance premiums for USAA term life policies: $250,000 death benefit for a male nonsmoker.

Age	Annual Renewable Term	10-Year Level Term	15-Year Level Term	20-Year Level Term
25	$ 250.00	$ 280.00	$ 310.00	$ 330.00
30	250.00	287.50	317.50	342.50
35	260.00	290.00	322.50	355.00
40	312.50	312.50	365.00	405.00
45	460.00	360.00	435.00	552.50
50	820.00	500.00	650.00	752.50
55	1,122.50	770.00	997.50	1,025.00
60	1,687.50	1,247.50	1,542.50	1,777.50
65	3,072.50	2,087.50	2,707.50	N.A.

Source: USAA Life Insurance Company, Preferred Plus Rates.

USAA Life Insurance Company, certainly among the lowest-cost and best life insurance companies in America, are shown in Exhibit 2-11. Fidelity Investments also has a life insurance subsidiary with competitive rates. You can even check it out and submit an application on the Internet. If the Smiths were to buy 10-year term policies in the amounts indicated, their monthly premiums would be about $100, or 1.7 percent of their salaries.

These ways of providing for heirs are not mutually exclusive. You can choose any two or all three of them if you want. Depending on the size of your estate and your estate planning efforts, these actions may have gift or estate tax consequences, which reduce the amount that your heirs actually receive. The usual admonition to consult your estate planning attorney, accountant, or financial adviser applies.

WHY START EARLY?

Whether your goal is a new house, a college fund, a comfortable retirement, or a large estate, you are more likely to achieve it sooner if you start your investment program sooner. Taking advantage of time and the arithmetic of compounding is one of the smartest moves any investor can make.

A 25-year-old early starter who makes a $2,000 annual contribution to a tax-deferred account for 10 years and then stops making contributions will have a balance of $340,000 when she reaches age 65 (see Exhibit 2-12). In contrast, a delayed starter, who makes his first annual $2,000 contribution to his investment program when he is 35, and makes them for a total of 30 years, will have only $264,000 when he reaches 65. The late and very late starters, who wait until they are 45 or 55, respectively, to start their investment programs, must save much larger amounts each year to accumulate the same total balance as the 25-year-old by the time they reach 65. The arithmetic is correct, but the results often seem unbelievable. It really pays to be an early starter.

Exhibit 2-12. The benefits of saving and investing early.

	Early Starter	Delayed Starter	Late Starter	Very Late Starter
Starting age	25	35	45	55
Years contributed	10 ←——→ 30		20	10
Ending age	35	65	65	65
Annual savings	$2,000	$2,000	$6,375	$20,100
Total amount saved	$20,000	$60,000	$127,500	$201,000
Annual total return (tax deferred)	8.0%	8.0%	8.0%	8.0%
Total balance at age 65	$340,000 ←→ $264,000		$340,000	$340,000

If you are closer to age 65 than 25 and have not started your investment program, you have already missed an opportunity to take advantage of time and compounding. To achieve your objectives, you may have to play catch-up. Realistically, to do so means some combination of (1) saving a larger portion of your income, (2) investing with a higher level of risk in order to achieve higher returns, or (3) extending your time horizon by postponing your retirement date. If you discover that some combination of these moves will not help, you will have to lower your objectives.

As your salary increases over time, it is important to save the same percentage of your income each year rather than the same dollar amount. By following this approach, you will save an amount you can afford and keep up with inflation. These results are illustrated in Exhibit 2-13. A 26-year-old woman who saves $1,000 per year and invests the money to earn an annual return of 8 percent will have a portfolio of almost $280,000 at age 65. Alternatively, if her salary increases 4 percent per year and she maintains her 10 percent savings rate, thereby increasing the dollar amount saved each year, her portfolio at age 65 will be $457,000 per $10,000 of her current salary. If you can do the same, you will certainly enjoy the same results.

Exhibit 2-13. The benefits of saving a constant percentage of income (8% annual return).

Age	Constant Amount		Per $10,000 of Salary (4% Inflation)	Constant 10 Percent	
	Amount Saved	Year-End Value		Amount Saved	Year-End Value
26	$ 1,000	$ 1,080	$10,000	$ 1,000	$ 1,080
27	1,000	2,246	10,400	1,040	2,290
28	1,000	3,506	10,816	1,082	3,641
29	1,000	4,867	11,249	1,125	5,147
30	1,000	6,336	11,699	1,170	6,822
•	•	•	•	•	•
•	•	•	•	•	•
•	•	•	•	•	•
61	1,000	202,070	39,461	3,946	320,334
62	1,000	219,316	41,039	4,104	350,393
63	1,000	237,941	42,681	4,268	383,034
64	1,000	258,056	44,388	4,439	418,471
65	1,000	279,781	46,164	4,616	456,934
Totals	$40,000	$280,000		$95,000	$457,000

IGNORE LIFE EVENTS?

What if life events don't matter to you? If you are already wealthy, saving and investing to achieve certain life event goals may be irrelevant. With a large investment portfolio and considerable net worth, you may be able to pay for the costs of major life events out of your current assets or income. In that case, you may prefer not to set financial goals in life-event terms. Instead, your goals should involve performance and risk standards for your investment portfolio. Specifically, your goal might be to meet or outperform a market benchmark over a specified time horizon. For example, you may want your portfolio to outperform a composite market index weighted 60 percent in equities, 30 percent in bonds, and 10 percent in cash by at least 1.5 percentage points per year for the next 5 years. Better yet, you should take taxes and risk into account and establish a performance objective expressed in after-tax risk-adjusted terms. Naturally, you will want to consider trade-offs between wealth preservation and growth. (More about these goals in Chapters 3 and 4.)

SUMMARIZE FINANCIAL GOALS

Once you have identified the life events that are important to you, the next step is to express them in financial terms. Specify the size of the fund you will need, and when you will need it, to achieve each of your goals. Translate annual streams of income or expense into lump sums using compound interest arithmetic. For example, the Smiths need $72,000 in 10 years to pay for their son's college education. They also need a retirement fund of $959,000 in 20 years to provide the income they will need during retirement. Because some of their needs will be provided by other means, the net amount that they must generate from additional savings and new investments is considerably less.

Since the Smith's needs are many years in the future, they expect the specific amounts involved to change over time. The dif-

Exhibit 2-14. Summary of investor's financial goals: The Smith family, as of 12/31/XX.

A. Table of Life Event Goals

	House Down Payment	Children's College	Happy Retirement	Estate for Heirs	Totals
From exhibit(s)	2-1	2-3	2-6 & 2-9	2-10	
Gross amount needed (future $)		$72,000	$959,000		$1,031,000
Net amount needed (future $)		$56,400	$400,000		$456,400
When needed (years)		10	20		
Annual total return		8.0%	8.0%		
Current Portfolio					
Tax deferred			$69,000		$69,000
Taxable			51,000		51,000
Total portfolio			$120,000		$120,000
Current monthly salaries					$6,000
Required monthly savings					
Education IRA ($500 per year)		$42			$42
Roth IRA (2 × $2,000 per year)		333			333
Traditional IRA					
401(k) plan (≤ 15% of salaries)			$500		$500
Keogh account					
Other tax-deferred accounts					
Taxable accounts		50			50
Amount to save each month	$425	$500			$925
% of salaries	7.1%	8.3%			15.4%
Plus: Employer matching contributions	–	$180			$180
Amount to invest each month	$425	$680			$1,105
% of salaries	7.1%	11.3%			18.4%
Annual amount to invest					$13,000
Unused IRA & 401(k) opportunities	$0	$333			
% of salaries	0.0%	5.6%			

B. Goal Statements

Pay for College in 10 Years

• Save a total of $425 per month (currently 7.1% of salaries or $5,100 per year) for the next 10 years.
  - $42 to an Education IRA (maximum is $500 per year, actually funded by the Child Tax Credit)
  - $333 to two Roth IRA accounts (annual maximum is $2,000 per person)
  - $50 to a taxable account (invest in tax-efficient mutual funds and pay taxes out of salaries)

• Invest monthly savings at 8% annual return to produce a college fund of $56,400 in 10 years.

• Monitor progress of $4,000 in grandparents' account to be sure it grows at 8 percent per year to provide $8,600 by Chris's freshman year.

• As salaries increase, maintain dollar amount of monthly savings so that increases can be targeted for retirement accounts.

Retire and Enjoy Life in 20 Years

• Make contributions totaling $500 per month to 401(k) plans (currently 8.3% of salary and $6,000 per year); be sure to qualify for maximum employer matching contributions (50% of employee contributions up to 6% of salary).

• Invest portfolio of $120,000 at 8% return to grow $559,000 over the next 20 years; for taxable accounts, buy tax-efficient mutual funds and pay taxes out of salary.

• Invest 401(k) contributions at 8% per year to grow to $400,000 over the next 20 years.

• As salary increases, maintain savings equal to at least 8.3% of salaries to accumulate a larger retirement fund.

• Strive to increase 401(k) contributions to the maximum level—the lesser of 15% of salaries or the maximum amount permitted by tax laws—e.g., $10,000 in 1998. At present, could contribute another $333 per month, or 5.6% of salaries.

ferences will reflect (1) changes in their financial situation, (2) the success of their investment program, and (3) the influence of taxes, inflation rates, and other variables dictated by the overall economy and government policy.

Your goals summary should also indicate the expected return on investment for the funds needed for each goal and any amounts you have already accumulated toward each goal. Finally, you should specify the monthly savings required to achieve your goals and the type of accounts you plan to use: tax deferred or taxable. The Summary of Investor's Financial Goals, comprising both a table of life event goals and goal statements, is shown in Exhibit 2-14. The Smiths do not have a financial goal for every possible life event, and you do not need a goal for each event either. But you do need goal statements to provide a foundation for developing your investment portfolio.

Once you know when to expect major life events, how much money you will need for each event, and how much you must save and invest to accumulate that amount, you can focus on building your investment portfolio. The goal is to achieve the required portfolio size and return on investment within an acceptable level of risk.

3

DETERMINING PORTFOLIO MIX

How should your portfolio be divided among equities, fixed income securities, and cash reserves? The answer requires taking inventory of your financial situation and portraying that information in a helpful way. After considering the returns provided by different types of investments and some reference points for perspective, you should decide on your basic portfolio mix and its equity components. Finally, you should summarize your asset allocation targets to serve as a reference as you select the funds for your portfolio.

PREPARE YOUR INVESTOR'S BALANCE SHEET

The Investor's Balance Sheet, a special form of personal financial statement, provides a foundation for your efforts. It presents a complete picture of all your *assets* (things you own) and *liabilities* (amounts you owe) and thus of your *net worth* (assets minus liabilities). You may have completed such forms in the past—as part of a mortgage application, for example. If so, you should get them out; they will be helpful in preparing your new statement.

Your net worth, as shown on your Investor's Balance Sheet (see Exhibit 3-1), is the measure of your material wealth. The goal

Exhibit 3-1. Investor's balance sheet.

A. Smith family financial statement, 12/31/XX

William A. Smith and Bonnie J. Smith   **(650) 555-1234**
615 Marmaduke Way   **Fax: (650) 555-5678**
Los Altos, California 94024

Assets		Liabilities and Net Worth	
Cash in Banks		**Real estate mortgages**	
XYZ Bank—market rate account	$ 5,000	Primary residence	$125,000
XYZ Bank—checking account	3,000	Vacation cabin	50,000
Total cash in banks	**$ 8,000**	**Total mortgages**	**$175,000**
Cash-equivalent assets			
Money market fund—taxable	$ 17,000	**Bank loans (notes payable)**	**$ 0**
U.S. Treasury bill—9 months	12,000		
XYZ Bank—6-month CD	8,000		
Total cash equivalents	**$ 37,000**	**Life insurance loans**	**$ 0**
% of investment portfolio	(31%)		
Fixed income assets (Part B)			
Bond mutual funds	$ 25,500	**Miscellaneous accounts and**	
Fixed income retirement funds	19,000	**credit cards**	**$ 4,000**
Cash Value—life insurance	6,500		
Total fixed income assets	**$ 51,000**		
% of investment portfolio	(42%)	**Income taxes payable**	**$ 3,600**
Equity assets (Part B)			
Equity retirement funds	$ 13,500	**Property taxes payable**	
Mutual funds—taxable	10,500	Primary residence	$ 1,600
Common stocks	8,000	Vacation cabin	800
Total equity assets	**$ 32,000**	**Total property taxes**	**$ 2,400**
% of investment portfolio	(27%)		
Total investment portfolio	**($120,000)**	**Total liabilities**	**$185,000**
Real Estate			
Primary residence			**Your**
(bought 6/30/9X)	$155,000	(Total assets − total liabilities)	**Wealth**
Vacation cabin (bought 9/30/8X)	70,000		
Total real estate	**$225,000**		
		Net worth	**($175,000)**
Personal property (market value)	**$ 7,000**		
Total assets	**$360,000**	**Total liabilities and net worth**	**$360,000**

(Part B is on page 58)

of your investment program should be to build your net worth over time so that you can achieve your financial goals. This financial statement provides a clear and comprehensive picture of net worth and its key components.

FOLLOW PRESCRIBED FORMAT

The balance sheet takes into account all your assets and liabilities in a form that is most useful for setting investment goals and monitoring progress toward building your investment portfolio and increasing your net worth. You can use any good spreadsheet program or a pencil, paper, and calculator to create your own.

The Investor's Balance Sheet highlights the investment portfolio and its three important components: cash-equivalent assets (CDs, money market funds, Treasury bills), fixed income assets (bonds), and equity assets (common stocks). Unfortunately, most people do not segregate their assets in this way.

The "cash in banks" category differs from the cash-equivalent assets shown as part of the investment portfolio. It includes the checking account that you use to write most of your checks. Your monthly paycheck probably is deposited to this account. This category may also include a market rate account with limited check-writing privileges and a slightly higher interest rate. You should maintain a combined balance of about one month's income in these two operating accounts. In contrast, your cash-equivalent assets are held primarily for investment purposes or as emergency reserves. They involve larger balances and earn higher rates of interest.

Many people don't have a personal financial statement at all, much less one that includes all of their assets. One of my clients, a doctor, was forever discovering a CD here, a bond fund there, or his wife's IRA account somewhere else. With a complete statement, individual investment decisions can be made within the context of the overall investment picture rather than on a piecemeal basis.

The financial statement should be limited to one page. A second page should be used to provide details of the investment portfolio. It should also show the breakdown between taxable accounts

Exhibit 3-1. Investor's balance sheet *(continued)*.

B. Smith family financial statement, 12/31/XX:
Details of investment portfolio

Assets	Taxable Accounts	Tax-Advantaged Accounts	Total Portfolio
Money market fund	$17,000	$0	$ 17,000
U.S. Treasury bill—9 months	12,000	0	12,000
XYZ Bank—6-month CD	8,000	0	8,000
Cash-equivalent assets	**$37,000**	**$0**	**$ 37,000**
% of investment portfolio			**31%**
American Century–Benham GNMA	$0	$13,500	$ 13,500
Vanguard Short-Term Corporate	0	12,000	12,000
Bond mutual funds	$0	$25,500	$ 25,500
Guaranteed investment contract	$0	$14,000	$ 14,000
U.S. Treasury note	0	5,000	5,000
Fixed income retirement funds	$0	$19,000	$ 19,000
ABC Mutual Life Insurance	$0	$ 4,000	$ 4,000
Trans Global Insurance	0	2,500	2,500
Cash value—life insurance	$0	$ 6,500	$ 6,500
Fixed income assets	**$0**	**$51,000**	**$ 51,000**
% of investment portfolio			**42%**
Fidelity Equity Income II	$ 7,500	$0	$ 7,500
William Blair Growth Fund	3,500	3,000	6,500
Longleaf Partners Small Cap Fund	0	6,000	6,000
Neuberger & Berman Partners	0	4,000	4,000
Domestic stock funds	**$11,000**	**$13,000**	**$ 24,000**
First National Bancorp	$3,000	$0	$3,000
Heavy Metal Manufacturing	0	3,000	3,000
Big Retail Stores	0	2,000	2,000
Common stocks	**$ 3,000**	**$ 5,000**	**$ 8,000**
Total equity assets	**$14,000**	**$18,000**	**$ 32,000**
% of investment portfolio			**27%**
Total investment portfolio	**$51,000**	**$69,000**	**$120,000**

and tax-advantaged accounts, such as IRAs, 401(k)s, and Keogh plans. An example of the second page is shown in Exhibit 3-1B.

USE MARKET VALUES

In preparing this statement, assets should be stated at their market values. Remember that the idea is to create a comprehensive picture of your financial situation—one that helps you, not one that will be presented to lenders—so there is no need to overstate asset values for items such as personal property. In fact, I believe that it is best to assign no value to such items as cars, boats, furniture, and jewelry. Because their true market values are hard to determine, their values and your net worth are likely to be overstated on the balance sheet and provide a false sense of wealth.

CALCULATE CURRENT ASSET MIX

Once the statement is complete, calculate your current asset mix. The Smiths found that their portfolio consists of 27 percent equity assets, 42 percent fixed income assets, and 31 percent cash-equivalent assets. Now you're ready to start making some decisions about your investment portfolio—specifically, to choose your target asset allocation.

ESTABLISH ASSET ALLOCATION TARGETS

Asset allocation involves determining how much of your portfolio should be invested in equities, fixed income securities, and cash equivalents. Why should you spend time figuring out your target asset allocation? Why not just get on with picking some great mutual funds that will make a lot of money? Research shows that a major portion of the return on investment of a diversified portfolio is attributable to how assets are allocated among these three categories rather than on individual stock or bond selection. Thus, the asset mix you choose may be one of your most important investment decisions, and it is a good way to begin constructing your portfolio.

Consider Expected Returns

During the past 70 years, stocks have returned an average of over 10 percent per year. Bonds have provided a total return of 5 to 6 percent, and short-term cash investments have yielded about 3 to 4 percent. (Just remember 10-6-4 as the returns on stocks, bonds, and cash, respectively.) At the same time, inflation, as measured by the CPI, has averaged about 3 percent per year. Clearly investors who

Exhibit 3-2. Average total returns of different types of securities for different time periods.

	Average Total Return (%)			
	70 Years, 1927–1996	50 Years, 1947–1996	25 Years, 1972–1996	10 Years, 1987–1996
Large company stocks (S&P 500 Index)	10.7%	12.6%	12.1%	15.3%
Small company stocks (DFA Small Company Fund)	12.8	14.4	15.5	13.0
Long-term corporate bonds (Salomon Brothers index)	5.6	5.8	9.2	9.5
Long-term government bonds (20-year maturity)	5.0	5.3	9.0	9.4
Intermediate-term gov. bonds (5-year maturity)	5.2	5.9	8.7	7.8
U.S. Treasury bills (30-day maturity)	3.7	4.9	7.0	5.5
Inflation (Consumer Price Index)	3.2	4.1	5.6	3.7

have chosen to hold a large portion of their portfolios in cash have had a false sense of security. Their returns have only slightly out-paced the level of inflation.

The average returns for the past 70, 50, 25, and 10 years are shown in Exhibit 3-2. For planning purposes, and to be conserva-tive, I have chosen to use the figures for 70 years as the expected annual rates of return in the future. If you want, you may use the figures for a shorter time period in your own calculations. The re-sult of such higher return on investment assumptions would be that you would need to save and invest less to achieve your finan-cial goals. You would also increase the risk that you would not achieve your financial goals.

Projecting the long-term average returns into the future, the weighted average return of a portfolio invested 60 percent in stocks, 30 percent in bonds, and 10 percent in cash equivalents is 8.4 percent. (Just remember 60-30-10.) See Exhibit 3-3. To be conser-vative, you should assume an 8 percent return in your calculations. This rate is also 4 percent over the expected rate of inflation. If you can achieve that level of return over an extended period of time, your portfolio should enable you to achieve your financial goals.

Exhibit 3-3. Weighted average total return: 60-30-10 portfolio.

Asset Category	Target Asset Allocation	×	1927–1996 Average Annual Return[a]	=	Weighted Average Return
Cash (T-bills)	10%		3.7%		0.4%
Bonds (intermediate term)	30		5.2		1.6
Stocks (S&P 500)	60		10.7		6.4
Total portfolio	100%			Total return % =	(8.4)

[a] Pretax total return, including interest, dividends, and capital appreciation.

The corresponding return based on results for the past 10 years would be 12 percent. Nevertheless, it is better to use the more conservative 8 percent return target. Then you can be pleased if actual returns are higher rather than disappointed if you choose a higher return target and actual results fall short of target levels. For example, it would be unrealistic and even irresponsible to use the unusually high 1995–1997 equity returns as a basis for projections for 5 to 10 years into the future. It is highly unlikely that such returns can be maintained over an extended period of time.

A shift in your asset allocation of 10 percentage points from stocks to bonds reduces the annual return by about 50 basis points. (A *basis point* is one-hundredth of 1 percent.) So a modest change results in a significant difference in the value of the portfolio over periods of 5, 10, 15, 20, or more years—the relevant time horizons for investors.

Why not just invest entirely in stocks, the category with the highest return? Because stocks are more volatile than bonds or cash. The average increase for large company stocks (the S&P 500) may have been more than 10 percent, but their annual results ranged from a gain of *plus* 50 percent to losses of *minus* 10 to 40 percent. These results are more volatile and thus riskier than bonds. In comparison, intermediate-term government bonds have had annual returns ranging from *plus* 30 percent to *minus* 5 percent. The longer the investor's time horizon and the higher the tolerance for risk, the more stocks the investor can comfortably hold. Moreover, stocks and bonds don't always move in the same direction. A balanced portfolio tends to have less volatility than one invested entirely in stocks.

As we grow older, our investment horizons become shorter, and we have less time to recover from any significant decline in market value. Thus, as we age, we should have less invested in higher-return and more volatile equities and more invested in less risky but lower-return fixed income securities.

REVIEW REFERENCE POINTS

Financial magazines such as *Money* and *Worth* and financial newsletters often have articles about asset allocation. They agree that the older you get, the less you should have in equity assets and the more in fixed income securities. At the same time, you need to find a way to help you determine the right mix for your portfolio based on your own situation, a very personal decision. Here are some helpful information sources and techniques.

• *Rule of thumb.* The first and easiest approach is to use a rule of thumb based on your age. The rule is that the percentage of your portfolio invested in equities should equal 110 minus your age. If you are 30, you should hold 80 percent in equities. If you are 60, you should have 50 percent in equities. A more conservative investor should use 100 minus his age as his rule, and a woman who is an aggressive investor should use 120 minus her age. All three of these formulas are illustrated in Exhibit 3-4. It shows that if you are 45 years old, like Bill Smith, 65 percent of your portfolio should be invested in equities. The remainder of the portfolio is divided between cash equivalents and fixed income investments.

• *Brokerage firm recommendations.* The recommended asset mix of major brokerage firms, including Merrill Lynch, Dean Witter, and Smith Barney, is often published in the *Wall Street Journal.* This

Exhibit 3-4. Asset allocation by rule of thumb.

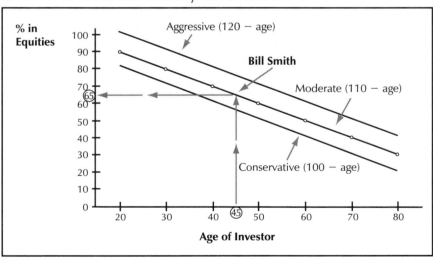

Source: From *Mutual Funds for Dummies®,* by Eric Tyson. Text © 1994, 1995, 1996, 1997 Eric Tyson. All rights reserved. Reproduced here by permission of IDG Books Worldwide, Inc. . . . For Dummies is a registered trademark under exclusive license to IDG Books Worldwide, Inc., from International Data Group, Inc.

mix reflects each firm's view of current market conditions and the outlook for each asset category. A recent example is shown in Exhibit 3-5. With one exception, the recommendations for each asset category are rounded to the nearest 5 percent, indicating that allocation is a matter of judgment and not a mathematically precise process. The average mix of 14 major firms included 56 percent in equities, with the range from 40 to 70 percent. This mix is for a growth-oriented investor, with no allowance made for differences in age, income level, size of portfolio, or financial goals.

Exhibit 3-5. Equity portion recommendations of 14 major brokerage firms.

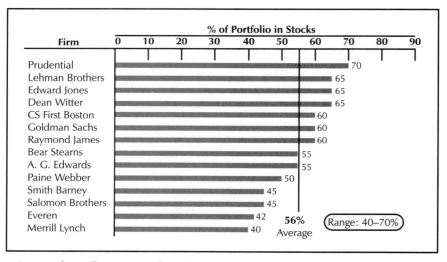

Source: The *Wall Street Journal,* April 30, 1997. Reprinted by permission of the *Wall Street Journal.* © 1997 Dow Jones & Company, Inc. All rights reserved worldwide.

• *Lifestyle funds.* Another approach is to make your allocation decision by mimicking the asset mix of the new "lifestyle funds" introduced by Stagecoach Funds, Vanguard, and Charles Schwab. These funds allocate the assets in each of their mutual funds according to the age or years to retirement of the investor (see Exhibit 3-6). For example, the Stagecoach fund designed for a 60-year-old with 5 years to retirement would have 25 percent in equities. An investor comfortable with the conservative growth objective of the

Exhibit 3-6. Equity portion of lifestyle mutual funds.

Stagecoach Lifepath Funds

Target Date	Assumed Age	% in Stocks
2000	60	25%
2010	50	50
2020	40	68
2030	30	80
2040	20	95

Schwab Asset Director Funds

Investment Objective	% in Stocks
Conservative growth	40%
Balanced growth	60
High growth	80

Vanguard Life Strategy Funds

Investment Objective	% in Stocks
Income	20%
Conservative growth	40
Moderate growth	60
Growth	80

Source: Fund prospectuses, annual reports.

Schwab or Vanguard funds might well choose a mix including 40 percent in equities.

DECIDE BASIC PORTFOLIO MIX

Most people are too conservative in their asset allocation. They have too much in cash reserves and fixed income securities and not enough in equities. This imbalance results from being risk averse and playing it safe on many individual investment decisions, each made in a vacuum rather than within the context of the entire portfolio. You should resolve not to make investment decisions in the future without knowing how they fit into your portfolio as a whole. The logical sequence for the steps involved in deciding your portfolio mix is shown in Exhibit 3-7.

Exhibit 3-7. Steps for deciding on a portfolio mix.

Step 1: A percentage in equities. The key choice in your asset mix decision is the percentage of your portfolio to be invested in equities. Equities have the greatest impact on whether you are able to achieve your portfolio goals. Over time, they have earned the highest average return and are the most volatile.

For many investors, equities also represent the largest portion of the portfolio. At least they should start as the largest portion and then gradually decline as the investor ages. For example, a 28-year-old, married with two children, with a steady income, and a portfolio of $100,000 adopted an asset mix with 80 percent in equities. A 75-year-old widower with a steady income stream independent of his investments and a $2.5 million portfolio chose to have 30 percent of his portfolio in equities. As shown in Exhibit 3-8, the Smith family examined the allocation indicated by each of the reference points outlined above and chose 60 percent in equities for its target mix.

Exhibit 3-8. Investor's choice: Percentage in equities.

Reference Point	% in Equities
Rule of Thumb, age 45	
Aggressive (120−age)	75%
Moderate (110−age)	65
Conservative (110−age)	55
Major brokerage firms (4/97)	
Average	56
Range	14–70
Lifestyle funds	
Stagecoach—2015/age 45	59
Schwab—balanced growth	60
Vanguard—moderate growth	60
Smith family choice	60%

Step 2: An amount in cash equivalents. Investors hold cash-equivalent assets in their portfolios to provide a cushion of readily available cash reserves that may be tapped in an emergency. For example, if the investor loses his job, this money can be used to pay living expenses until he is employed again. Fortunately, this pool may be tapped without having to sell assets at a loss in the event of a market downturn.

For many investors the *amount* of cash, rather than the percentage, is the key factor for determining the level of cash-equivalent assets in their portfolio. This amount depends on your level of job security, transferability of skills, and attitude toward risk. The amount of cash should equal 3 to 12 months' worth of your gross income. This amount will actually cover your expenses for a longer period of time because no income taxes will be due upon its withdrawal. You may want to choose an even larger amount if you are self-employed in a volatile business or are living off your investments and want to avoid selling equities when markets are down in order to make withdrawals.

The Smiths decided that it was unlikely that they would both be unemployed at the same time, so they chose to maintain a cushion equal to 5 months of their current monthly income (see Exhibit 3-9). They figured that this amount would cover more than 8 months of their expenses.

If the value of your portfolio is small compared to your income, the amount of cash that you hold is likely to be a higher percentage of your portfolio than would otherwise be the case. Alternatively, if your portfolio is large and your income and expenses relatively modest, you should increase the cash-equivalent portion of your portfolio. A rule that applies in a wide range of circumstances is to maintain cash equivalents equal to the larger of (1) a specified number of months of gross income or (2) 5 to 10 percent of your portfolio.

Step 3: The remainder in fixed income securities. The fixed income portion of the portfolio helps reduce volatility and maintain a steadier return on investment. After you have determined the equity percentage and cash amount of your portfolio, the remainder of the portfolio should be in fixed income securities. For the Smiths, the resulting target asset allocation was 60 percent in

Exhibit 3-9. Target asset allocation: The investor's decision.

	Smith Family	Your Figures
Current investment portfolio	$120,000	
Planned new investments in next 12 months (from Exhibit 2-14)	13,000	
A. Total investment portfolio in 12 months	$133,000	
Step 1: A percentage in equities		
B. Equity assets % of portfolio (Exhibit 3-8) ⇒	60%	
C. Target equity assets (A × B)	$ 80,000	
Step 2: An amount in cash equivalents		
D. Current monthly income	$ 6,000	
E. Times: Months of cash reserves (3−12) ⇒	5	
F. Equals: Target cash equivalents (D × E)	$ 30,000	
G. Cash equivalents % of portfolio (F ÷ A)	23%	
	(minimum=5 to 10%)	
Step 3: The remainder in fixed income securities		
H. Fixed income % of portfolio (100% − B − G)	17%	
I. Target fixed income assets (A × H)	$ 23,000	
Recap of target asset allocation % (equities–fixed income–cash equivalents)	60-17-23	
⇒ = **Your choice**		

equities, 17 percent in fixed income assets, and 23 percent in cash equivalents. Bill and Bonnie Smith just need to remember 60-17-23.

Reference points and analytical methods are helpful in determining portfolio mix by providing perspective, but they cannot provide a single correct answer. Your judgment is required to determine the mix that is best for you. Thus, you should decide on a specific mix and keep it firmly in mind as you make decisions regarding the components of the equity portion and then select specific investments within each asset category.

SPECIFY EQUITY COMPONENTS

Once you have chosen the basic asset mix, you need to determine the composition of the equity portion. Here you select the portion to be in (1) international equities, (2) an index or asset class fund, and (3) three to five actively managed funds, including an optional real estate fund. In an actively managed fund, the fund manager selects the stocks to own and the level of investment in each one. In contrast, the manager of an index fund simply owns all the stocks in the index in the same proportion as the index itself. In that sense, an index fund is "unmanaged" or "passively managed." Choosing the equity components involves applying judgment, simple arithmetic, and a logical sequence.

Following are the rest of the steps for deciding on your portfolio mix.

Step 4: A portion in international equities. First, choose a target for international equities. The U.S. share of the world's investments is shrinking. And, as shown in Exhibit 3-10, many of the world's stock markets have outperformed the U.S. market over the past 10 years. Since foreign equity markets often move in different directions and at different rates from U.S. markets, foreign investments provide greater diversification.

There is good support for the conclusion that 25 to 30 percent of the equity portion of your portfolio should be invested in foreign equities. The lifestyle funds sponsored by Charles Schwab and the Vanguard Group are designed to have 25 percent of the equity portion in international stocks. The allocation recommendations by

Exhibit 3-10. Compound annual returns in selected world stock markets, 10 years ending June 30, 1997.[a]

1. Hong Kong	19.9%
2. Netherlands	17.2%
3. Sweden	17.1%
4. Switzerland	16.8%
5. Denmark	15.7%
6. UNITED STATES	**15.0%**
7. Belgium	13.9%
8. Norway	10.8%
9. Australia	10.0%
10. Singapore	9.7%

[a]Compound annual returns, in U.S. dollars, with gross dividends reinvested.
Source: Morgan Stanley Capital International.

Bessemer Trust, Brown Brothers, Northern Trust, and Union Bank of Switzerland, as reported in the October 1997 issue of *Worth* magazine, range from 15 to 31 percent of equities in international stocks. This mix is intended for investors who are seeking long-term growth and total return.

Foreign stocks are riskier than U.S. stocks. At the very least, they may be subject to additional political risk and to currency risk. Nevertheless, research shows that an equity portfolio with 30 percent in international stocks and 70 percent in domestic issues provides a higher return and less risk exposure than a portfolio invested entirely in domestic stocks. This result is shown in Exhibit 3-11. As foreign stocks are added to a portfolio of domestic stocks, the total return increases and the risk is reduced until 30 percent of the portfolio is invested in foreign stocks. Then, as more foreign stocks are added, the return continues to increase, but additional risk is assumed. An individual investor with a well-chosen mix of domestic and international stock funds is likely to enjoy higher overall returns than an investor who holds only domestic stock funds.

Exhibit 3-11. Best foreign and domestic stock mix.

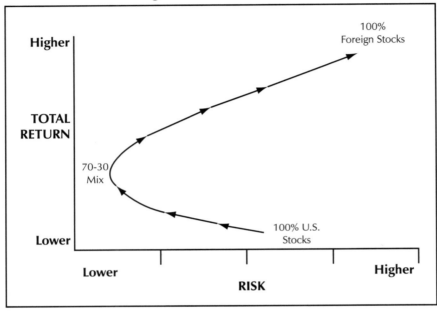

After considering the relevant reference points, the Smith family chose to commit 25 percent of its equity holdings to international equities in the form of foreign stock funds (see Exhibit 3-12). If the equity portion is targeted at 60 percent of the total portfolio, and 25 percent of the equity portion ought to be in international stocks, then 15 percent (25% × 60% = 15%) of the overall portfolio should be targeted for international equities. As shown in Exhibit 3-13, you should select the target percentage to be in international funds and then derive the corresponding dollar amount. Calculations for the Smith family are shown in column 1 of the exhibit. You can do your own calculations in the second column.

If you are uncertain about what percentage to choose, start with 25 percent of your equities in international funds, and continue the asset allocation process. Since domestic funds often hold about 5 percent in international stocks, you will end up with 30

Exhibit 3-12. Investor's choice: Percentage in international equities.

Reference Point	International Equities	
	% of Equities	% of Portfolio
Major brokerage firms (4/97)		
Average	24%	12%
Range	15–35	8–15
Lifestyle funds		
Schwab—balanced growth	25	15
Vanguard—moderate growth	25	15
Best foreign and domestic stock mix		
(Exhibit 3-11)	30	—
Worth magazine (10/97)		
Union Bank of Switzerland	31	20
Bessemer Trust	25	18
Northern Trust	15	13
Brown Brothers	15	10
Smith family choice	**25%**	**15%**

percent in international equities. You can revisit your choice and make adjustments after you have completed designing the entire portfolio and inspecting the results.

Step 5: Retained domestic stocks. The domestic portion of the portfolio comprises any common stocks you currently own and wish to retain and equity mutual funds. Subtract the dollar value of the common stocks from the total target for domestic equities to derive the target amount for domestic equity mutual funds.

The Smiths chose to have 25 percent of equities in international mutual funds and to keep the $8,000 they have in individual common stocks. As a result, their target for domestic equity mutual funds is $52,000.

Step 6: An index or asset class fund. Index funds can be excellent core holdings for any portfolio. These popular funds match the performance of the well-known market indexes, such as the

Exhibit 3-13. Components of target equity assets.

	Smith Family	Your Figures
A. Target equity assets (Exhibit 3-9)	$80,000	
Step 4: A portion in international equities		
B. International mutual funds % of equities ⇒	25%	⬭
C. Target international mutual funds (A × B)	$20,000	
Step 5: Retained domestic stocks		
D. Target domestic equities (A − C)	$60,000	
E. Less: Individual common stocks (if any) ⇒	($8,000)	⬭
F. Target domestic equity mutual funds (D − E)	$52,000	
Step 6: An index or asset class fund	25, 40, 55, or 70%	
G. % of domestic equity mutual funds ⇒	25%	⬭
H. Target index fund (F × G)	$13,000	
Step 7: A few actively managed funds		
I. Target in actively managed funds (F − H)	$39,000	
J. % in actively managed funds (100% − G)	75%	
K. Target number of funds (3, 4, or 5) ⇒	5	⬭
L. Portion in each fund (J ÷ K)	15% (minimum = 10%)	
M. Target amount in each fund (I ÷ K)	$7,800	
⇒ = Your choice		

S&P 500 Index, which contains the 500 largest domestic stocks. In fact, an S&P 500 Index fund will own each of the 500 stocks in the same proportion as the index itself.

By owning an index fund, you won't outperform the market, but you won't fall short of market performance either. Actually, that's a good accomplishment because the record shows that it is very difficult for active fund managers to outperform index funds. According to Vanguard, more than half of them beat the S&P 500 Index only three times in the decade ending December 31, 1995. During the same period, the Wilshire 5000 Index, a measure of the entire domestic U.S. stock market, outpaced more than half of the general equity funds in 8 of the 10 years. For the entire period, it outperformed 65 percent of these funds.

The so-called *asset class funds* are a variation on the index fund concept. Like index funds, they are passively managed—that is, they do not try to select individual stocks. Rather than tracking an index, they seek to provide broad exposure to a particular class of assets—for example, small companies that are undervalued, as indicated by a high book-value-to-market ratio. Some of these funds accomplish their goal by investing in all companies on the New York, American, and NASDAQ stock exchanges that meet the class criteria. The best asset class funds, particularly those devoted to small-cap value stocks, are offered by Dimensional Fund Advisors (DFA) and sold only through independent investment advisers.

Both index and asset class funds have very low expenses, low turnover, and low capital gains subject to taxation. In addition, they provide a benchmark against which to compare the performance of your other holdings. For these reasons, the pension funds of many corporations and public agencies, as well as many individual investors, have major commitments to these types of funds.

Accordingly, you should commit a substantial portion of your investment in domestic stock funds to an S&P 500 index or asset class fund. I recommend 25, 40, 55, or 70 percent, with the higher percentages being the more conservative choices. If you are unsure what level is best for you, start with 55 percent. The Smith family elected to be very aggressive and put only 25 percent (or $13,000) of its target for domestic equity mutual funds into an S&P 500 index fund.

Step 7: A few actively managed funds. The remainder of your commitment to domestic equity mutual funds should be in three, four, or five actively managed funds, with at least 10 percent in each fund. You use the index fund as the "core" of your portfolio and use actively managed funds with different characteristics to "explore" ways to outperform the market. Schwab calls this combination the Core & Explore™ approach. The *core* of your portfolio is certain to match the return of the underlying market index, while the *explore* portion provides further diversification and may be aimed at trying to beat the index fund on an absolute or risk-adjusted basis.

The Smiths chose to have five actively managed funds with 15 percent of their commitment to domestic equity mutual funds, or $7,800, invested in each fund. The target number of funds, the percentage in each fund, and the target dollar amount to be invested in each fund are also shown earlier in Exhibit 3-13.

Step 8: An optional real estate fund. Many investment advisers think that some real estate should be included in a well-diversified portfolio. Real estate provides further diversification because it is not directly correlated with the stock and bond markets. Real estate performance reflects the economy as a whole (e.g., interest rates, inflation, and economic growth), in addition to the local real estate market's supply and demand situation. According to Morningstar, the correlation between price movements of real estate mutual funds and the S&P 500 Index is low, thus confirming that a real estate fund will increase your portfolio's diversification.

Diversification may also be achieved within the real estate portion of your portfolio. Your real estate investment should include different types of properties, such as apartments, office buildings, hotels, storage facilities, and various other commercial properties. And since real estate markets tend to be local, it should include properties in different parts of the country.

A good way to invest in real estate markets is to buy a mutual fund that owns shares in real estate investment trusts (REITs). These funds own shares in REITs just like other funds own the common stock of other types of companies. REITs are professionally managed firms that specialize in developing and managing real estate properties. By owning funds that invest in REITs, you also get liquidity. You can sell the funds any time with a telephone call—a desirable feature you could not get in a limited partnership or with direct ownership of a small office complex, apartment, or duplex. You also avoid the headaches of being a landlord or developer.

A real estate mutual fund should comprise 5 or 10 percent of the portfolio as a whole. Like an international stock fund and an equity index fund, it should be regarded as part of the equity portion of your portfolio. It is one of your three to five actively managed funds. In a portfolio with an asset mix of 60-30-10, it is part of the 60 percent equity component. At least one brokerage house, Raymond James, routinely recommends that 5 or 10 percent of the total portfolio should be invested in real estate.

HOW MANY FUNDS?

One international fund, one market index fund, and three to five well-chosen actively managed funds will provide you with a well-diversified portfolio, including stocks that are not part of the S&P 500 Index. The goal is to achieve diversification but not to buy so many funds that you have bought the entire market. In that case, you might as well buy the Vanguard Total Stock Market Index Fund, which tracks the Wilshire 5000 Index, and leave it at that.

Over time, there is a natural tendency to add new funds to

Exhibit 3-14. Summary of asset allocation targets.

Asset Type	From Exhibit	The Smith Family Amount	% of Portfolio	Your Figures Amount	% of Portfolio
		(enter)	(calculate)	(enter)	(calculate)
Cash-equivalent assets	3-9	$ 30,000	23%		
Fixed income assets	3-9	23,000	17%		
Equity assets					
International mutual fund	3-13	20,000	15		
Individual common stocks	3-13	8,000	6		
An S&P 500 Index fund	3-13	13,000	10		
Actively managed funds	3-13	39,000	29		
Domestic equity mutual funds		52,000	39		
Total equity assets	3-9	80,000	60%		
Total investment portfolio	3-9	$133,000	100%		100%

your portfolio without removing old ones. The capital gains tax tends to lock you in to funds in the taxable portion of your portfolio. Thus, you should start with the smallest number of funds that will give you satisfactory diversification. With a total of five to seven funds, including an index fund with 500 stocks and at least 100 stocks in each actively managed fund, you will get plenty of diversification. If your funds owned none of the same stocks, you would have investments in at least 1,000 stocks and thus be well diversified by investment style, company size, and geographic region. There is no need to add more funds to increase diversification.

SUMMARIZE ASSET ALLOCATION TARGETS

After making choices for each category of the equity portion, you should summarize your target allocation as shown in Exhibit 3-14. Enter the dollar amount for each asset type, and then calculate its corresponding percentage of the total portfolio. The Smith family's targets coincide with its basic 60-17-23 mix and the equity components specified earlier in this chapter. By following the prescribed approach, you have determined the basic structure of your portfolio in a totally objective manner, without picking either specific funds or fund characteristics. Now you are ready to choose the characteristics of the funds you want in each of the categories you have just determined.

4

Choosing Stock Fund Characteristics

Selecting mutual funds is a challenge because there are so many of them. The best approach begins by specifying the characteristics of the funds you want to own. Then you can screen funds, using both analytical methods and common sense, to see how well they meet your criteria.

My mutual fund screening criteria and the logic flow for this chapter are shown in Exhibit 4-1. I discuss each of the screening criteria, the goal each is intended to achieve, and either how to achieve them or what key performance measures to use in evaluating funds. Various other exhibits illustrate how to home in on the best funds and provide worksheets for you to use.

Choose No-Load Funds

You should select only true no-load funds. That means no front-end loads, deferred charges, or 12b-1 fees. *Morningstar No-Load Funds* includes funds with loads of 3 percent or less and funds with 12b-1 fees, so you need to check the loads on each fund you consider. Each fund is reviewed and analyzed on a single page. An

Exhibit 4-1. Mutual fund screening criteria.

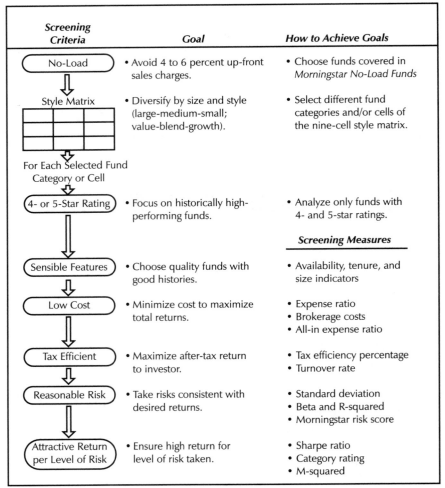

Screening Criteria	Goal	How to Achieve Goals
No-Load	• Avoid 4 to 6 percent up-front sales charges.	• Choose funds covered in *Morningstar No-Load Funds*
Style Matrix	• Diversify by size and style (large-medium-small; value-blend-growth).	• Select different fund categories and/or cells of the nine-cell style matrix.
For Each Selected Fund Category or Cell		
4- or 5-Star Rating	• Focus on historically high-performing funds.	• Analyze only funds with 4- and 5-star ratings.
		Screening Measures
Sensible Features	• Choose quality funds with good histories.	• Availability, tenure, and size indicators
Low Cost	• Minimize cost to maximize total returns.	• Expense ratio • Brokerage costs • All-in expense ratio
Tax Efficient	• Maximize after-tax return to investor.	• Tax efficiency percentage • Turnover rate
Reasonable Risk	• Take risks consistent with desired returns.	• Standard deviation • Beta and R-squared • Morningstar risk score
Attractive Return per Level of Risk	• Ensure high return for level of risk taken.	• Sharpe ratio • Category rating • M-squared

example of this Morningstar page is shown in Exhibit 4-2, which also highlights the items that you should use as selection criteria for domestic stock funds. Review this page carefully. The Morningstar page is your principal source of information about an individual mutual fund. Your task is to use the information on these pages to identify the funds you want to evaluate further and then to screen those funds against the selection criteria.

Exhibit 4-2. Morningstar page: William Blair Growth fund.

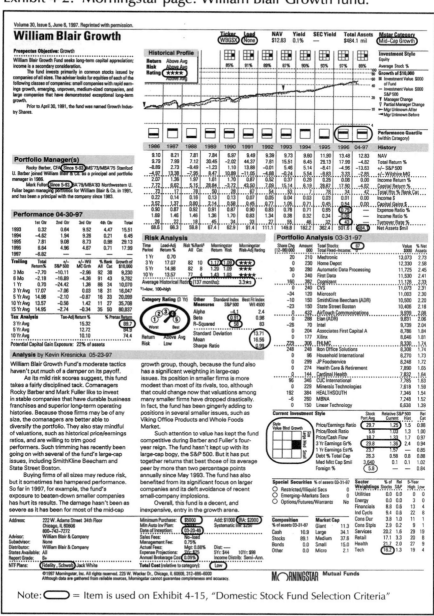

Note: ⬭ = Item is used on Exhibit 4-15, "Domestic Stock Fund Selection Criteria"

Source: Reprinted with permission of Morningstar.

Specify Desired Investment Styles

The next characteristic you should choose involves a fund's Morningstar category and investment style. Your goal should be to select different categories of funds so that your portfolio will be diversified and thus have a reasonable level of risk.

Ignore Prospectus Objective

Standard practice in the mutual fund industry has been to classify funds according to the investment objective spelled out in their prospectuses. Thus, domestic equity funds may be classified as aggressive growth, growth, growth & income, equity-income, small company, and sector funds. These labels indicate the kind of companies in which the funds invest. Slightly different categories, developed by Lipper Analytical Services, are used by the *Wall Street Journal* in reporting mutual fund performance.

One weakness in this classification system is that mutual funds often label themselves one way in their prospectus and then behave in quite another. For example, an equity-income fund might take on the additional risk of investing in growth stocks in order to increase its overall return. In that case, the equity-income label would be inconsistent with the fund's actual practices. An investor relying on that classification would be misled.

It is best to ignore the prospectus objectives, since funds with the same objective may actually be managed with very different styles, and those with different objectives may actually have portfolios with similar characteristics. In short, these labels are unreliable for use in selecting funds to be part of a diversified portfolio.

Use Investment-Style Matrix

To overcome this shortcoming, Morningstar uses a nine-cell style matrix based on the actual behavior and performance of the funds. The matrix for equity funds is shown in Exhibit 4-3. Its dimensions are explained in every edition of *Morningstar No-Load Funds* on the inside of the last page of the Summary Section.

The vertical axis of the equity-style matrix is the median mar-

Exhibit 4-3. Morningstar's equity-style matrix.

Risk		Investment Style			Size[a]
		Value	Blend	Growth	
Low	○	Large-cap Value	Large-cap Blend	Large-cap Growth	Large
Moderate	◐	Mid-cap Value	Mid-cap Blend	Mid-cap Growth	Medium
High	●	Small-cap Value	Small-cap Blend	Small-cap Growth	Small

[a]"Size" is median market capitalization.

Source: Morningstar No-Load Funds.

ket capitalization in billions of dollars of the companies owned by the fund. A company's total *market capitalization* is its price per share times the number of shares that it has outstanding. Not surprisingly, the three size levels are called large (or large-cap), medium (or mid-cap), and small (or small-cap). *Large-cap funds* are those with median market capitalizations of more than $5 billion. *Mid-cap funds* have median market capitalizations between $1 billion and $5 billion, and *small-cap funds* have median market capitalizations of less than $1 billion.

The horizontal axis shows whether the investment approach of the fund is value oriented, growth oriented, or a blend of value and growth. A *value fund* looks for bargains; it buys stocks that it regards as undervalued. A *growth fund* manager buys stock of companies whose earnings are expected to grow significantly in the future. Morningstar determines the actual style of each fund analytically by comparing the fund's average price-earnings (P/E) ratio and price-book ratio to the levels for the S&P 500 Index. Both the absolute and relative levels of these ratios are reported on the Morningstar page for each fund. Growth funds have above-average ratios, and value funds have below-average ratios. The three styles are called *value, blend,* and *growth.*

The result is a matrix with three values on each axis—a nine-cell matrix. Every stock mutual fund falls into one of the cells. Under this system, a domestic fund may be classified according to size and style: large-cap value, mid-cap blend, small-cap growth, and so forth. As if to confirm the shortcomings of prospectus objectives, the large-value and mid-cap value categories include funds with objectives of growth, growth & income, and equity-income.

Morningstar uses 18 categories for domestic equity funds: 9 for diversified funds and 9 for specialty funds that concentrate on specific industry sectors. You should focus on the diversified funds. They are assigned to categories based on their prevalent style for the previous 3 years. These categories have the same names as the cells in the style matrix. Here they are, along with their abbreviations:

LV Large-cap Value	LB Large-cap Blend	LG Large-cap Growth
MV Mid-cap Value	MB Mid-cap Blend	MG Mid-cap Growth
SV Small-cap Value	SB Small-cap Blend	SG Small-cap Growth

The current investment style for a domestic equity fund may differ from its category. Thus, a fund in Morningstar's mid-cap blend category may have a large-growth style. In such a case, the fund has experienced style drift, perhaps as a result of an increase in median market capitalization caused by an overall increase in market values or by a conscious shift by the fund manager. In building your portfolio, you should rely on a fund's investment style, since that is the best indication of the fund's current holdings. To make comparisons with other funds, consider the fund to be in another category based on its current investment style.

SET PERCENTAGE IN EACH STYLE CELL

To design your portfolio, first decide on the percentage of your investment in domestic equity mutual funds that you want in each cell of the nine-cell matrix. An S&P 500 index fund belongs in the large-cap blend (LB) cell. A real estate fund belongs in the small-cap value (SV) cell. However, you should not regard the SV cell covered unless it contains a diversified equity fund. Other actively managed funds should be sprinkled into other cells to achieve the desired emphasis and diversification. Of course, there are plenty of possible alternatives, and you don't need to have a fund in each cell.

The nine examples shown in Exhibit 4-4 are intended to illus-

Exhibit 4-4. Examples of domestic fund allocations.

1 index fund + 3 A/M funds

70% Index / Value

	Value	Blend	Growth	
Large		(70)		70%
Medium	10	10		20%
Small	10			10%
	20%	80%	0%	

55% Index / Blend

	Value	Blend	Growth	
Large		(55)		55%
Medium	15		15	30%
Small		15		15%
	15%	70%	15%	

40% Index / Growth

	Value	Blend	Growth	
Large		(40)		40%
Medium			20	20%
Small		20	20	40%
	0%	60%	40%	

1 index fund + 4 A/M funds

55% Index / Value

	Value	Blend	Growth	
Large	10	(55)		65%
Medium	10			10%
Small	10		15	25%
	30%	55%	15%	

40% Index / Blend

	Value	Blend	Growth	
Large	15	(40)		55%
Medium	15		15	30%
Small			15	15%
	30%	40%	30%	

25% Index / Growth

	Value	Blend	Growth	
Large		(25)		25%
Medium		20	20	40%
Small	20		15	35%
	20%	45%	35%	

1 index fund + 5 A/M funds

40% Index / Blend

	Value	Blend	Growth	
Large	12	(40)		52%
Medium	12	12	12	36%
Small			12	12%
	24%	52%	24%	

25% Index / Value

	Value	Blend	Growth	
Large	15	(25)		40%
Medium	15	15	15	45%
Small	15			15%
	45%	40%	15%	

↑
(SELECTED BY THE SMITH FAMILY)

50% Index / Growth

	Value	Blend	Growth	
Large		(50)	10	60%
Medium		10	10	20%
Small	10		10	20%
	10%	60%	30%	

Note: A/M = actively managed fund.
○ = index fund.

trate different patterns. They are labeled to indicate the relative size of the S&P 500 index fund portion (25, 40, 55, or 70 percent) and whether the other cells selected provide a growth or value emphasis. They also indicate the relative concentration on funds that invest in large, medium, and small companies. Through trial and error, you should be able to develop a pattern that is comfortable to you. A value emphasis will lead you to select funds that own lower-priced value stocks. A growth emphasis will lead you to choose growth funds with higher potential returns and a greater level of risk.

The Smith family had previously elected to have 25 percent in an index fund and 15 percent in each of five actively managed funds. They now decided to allocate their actively managed funds to achieve a value emphasis: 45 percent in value funds, 40 percent in blend funds, and 15 percent in growth funds. They like value funds rather than growth funds with a greater potential for price declines if earnings targets are not achieved. They also chose to have 40 percent in large-cap stocks, 45 percent in mid-caps, and 15 percent in small-cap stocks. This mix gives them good diversification by size of company so that their portfolio will perform well regardless of whether the market favors large or small companies.

Once you have determined the percentage you want in each cell, multiply those percentages by the total target amount for domestic equity mutual funds to derive the dollar amount to be invested in funds that fall into each cell. This approach is shown in Exhibit 4-5. After you have completed this step, you are ready to specify the criteria to be used to select funds within each investment category.

ADOPT FUND SELECTION CRITERIA

The criteria for selecting funds are quite simple. You want no-load funds with four- or five-star ratings. You want funds that have basic features that make good common sense, that are low cost and tax efficient, with a reasonable level of risk and an attractive return for the risk that they assume.

Exhibit 4-5. Domestic equity mutual fund-style targets.

	Value	Blend	Growth	
Target Total Amount = $52,000				
Large	(15%) $7,800	(25%) $13,000		40%
Medium	(15%) $7,800	(15%) $7,800	(15%) $7,800	45%
Small	(15%) $7,800			15%
	45%	40%	15%	

$52,000	Target total amount
× 15%	Percentage in small-value funds
$7,800	Target amount for small-value funds

START WITH FOUR- AND FIVE-STAR RATINGS

Morningstar, which has become the oracle on mutual fund performance and characteristics during the past several years, rates funds on a scale of 1 to 5 stars, based on their historical performance, with 5 being the best. These ratings take into account the fund's return and its risk compared to other funds.

To determine the star rating, each fund's relative risk score (average = 1.00) is subtracted from its relative return score (average = 1.00). The resulting figure is compared to that of all other domestic stock funds. The top 10 percent are assigned a 5-star rating, the next 22.5 percent a 4-star rating, and so forth. Thus, the 4- and 5-star ratings represent the top one-third of the nearly 700 no-load funds that Morningstar follows. Stars are assigned for 3-, 5-, and 10-year periods.

You should choose only 4- and 5-star funds for further analysis. Although some funds have maintained an average rating of 4 stars for 10 years or more, the number of stars is not intended to be a predictor of future performance. Nevertheless, it seems logical to begin with funds that have had comparatively good risk-adjusted performance in the past, especially since the star ratings are not the only criteria to be used. Ignoring these ratings or selecting funds with poor ratings certainly doesn't make any sense.

CHOOSE SENSIBLE FEATURES

In addition to high-performance ratings, your funds should have solid fundamental characteristics, including reasonable longevity, adequate diversification, and manageable size. Naturally, they should have comfortable minimum purchase requirements for individual investors and be available with little or no transaction fees through your discount broker. Specifically, they should have these characteristics:

• *Available through a discount broker.* With an account at Schwab, Fidelity, Vanguard, or another discount brokerage firm, you will get the advantage of low or no commissions and the convenience of a single monthly statement. These firms publish lists of the funds they offer, and Morningstar identifies which brokers offer the fund with no transaction fees (NTF) on each fund's Morningstar page. Most of the funds are available to you directly as an individual account holder, although some excellent funds are offered only through independent investment advisers.

• *Affordable to the individual investor.* The fund should have minimum purchase requirements within your reach as an individual investor. I use $3,000 or less for initial investments in taxable amounts and no more than $500 for subsequent investments. These amounts are smaller for IRA accounts. If you do not already own the fund, it should also be open to new investors. Many good-performing funds, especially those that focus on small companies, close to new investors because they find it difficult to maintain their investment style if huge amounts of cash pour in to the fund. They generally reopen in the future.

• *Five-year track record.* This standard may rule out some good newer funds, including start-up funds. Nevertheless, choosing a fund with a performance record of at least 5 years is preferable and prudent, given the wide range of choices available.

• *Consistent management.* The fund should have the same manager(s) who achieved the good performance record. Otherwise the track record has little meaning. Long tenures are better than short ones, and tenure of at least 3 years is mandatory.

• *Reasonable size.* The funds should have total assets of at least $200 million and be small enough to be nimble in the marketplace. Although some giant funds have performed well in recent years, I still prefer a fund, other than an index or asset class fund, to have assets of no more than $5 billion. Larger funds tend to be unwieldy and gravitate toward the performance of the market as a whole.

• *A portfolio of 50 to 200 stocks.* About 100 stocks is probably ideal. It's hard for me to imagine a portfolio manager really staying on top of more than 100 stocks. Of course, this limitation and many of the other criteria do not apply to index or asset class funds.

FAVOR LOW-COST FUNDS

What are a mutual fund's costs, and why are they important to investors? No-load mutual funds, like other businesses, have both revenues and expenses. They charge a management fee, usually related to asset size and sometimes linked to performance as well. Morningstar reports both the fee arrangement and actual management fees. Other expenses include 12b-1 fees, used to pay a fund's marketing and distribution-related costs, trustees' fees, and all other operating expenses. These costs are not reported separately but are included with management fees in a total expense ratio: total expenses as a percentage of net assets.

The average domestic stock fund has an expense ratio of about 140 basis points, or 1.4 percent of assets under management. Some funds have expenses of 250 basis points or more. These costs come right out of your pocket and reduce the total return of the fund. Thus, I prefer stock funds with expenses of 100 basis points or less. The lowest-cost funds are from Vanguard, which has many funds with annual expenses of 30 basis points or less.

Funds also incur brokerage costs when they buy and sell securities. Naturally, these costs are higher for funds with lots of transactions and lower for those with little trading activity. These costs are not included in the expense ratio. Morningstar reports the brokerage costs as a separate ratio, which you may add to the expense ratio to derive an "all-in" cost ratio. For example, a fund with an expense ratio of 1.00 percent and brokerage costs of 0.35 percent would have an all-in cost ratio of 1.35 percent, a better measure of the fund's true costs than the expense ratio alone.

Some people assert that a mutual fund's costs are not important. They argue that what really matters is the fund's total return on investment. It is tempting to accept that logic, until you realize it is false.

A mutual fund's *total return* is the result of its price appreciation, interest, dividends, *and* costs. Thus, the total return figures reported in newspapers are net of expenses. Within reason, if the costs were lower, the returns would be correspondingly higher. Moreover, fund management has more control over costs than over other components of total return. It is easier to cut costs than to increase growth, interest, or dividends.

• *Costs related to assets.* Fund costs seem low when they are expressed as a percentage of assets—for example, 1.40 percent (140 basis points). Direct brokerage costs may add another 10 basis points for a fund with little turnover and 50 basis points for a fund with lots of transactions. Thus, a fund's all-in cost ratio could easily be 200 basis points or more. The all-in expense ratio and its components for selected mutual funds are shown in Exhibit 4-6. Although all of the funds in the exhibit have below-average expense ratios, the range in costs is striking. The all-in costs of the higher-cost funds are several times that of the funds with the lowest costs.

• *Costs as a percentage of total return.* It's all right to quote fees and expenses as a percentage of assets. However, you should also look at total costs as a percentage of the fund's total return. This

Exhibit 4-6. Annual mutual fund costs as a percentage of total fund assets, ranked by all-in expense ratio.

Mutual Fund	(1) Actual Management Fee	(2) +Other Costs	(3) Reported = Expense Ratio	(4) Annual + Brokerage Costs[a]	(5) All-In =Expense Ratio
Source or Calculation	(enter)	(3 − 1)	(enter)	(enter)	(3 + 4)
Vanguard Short-Term Corporate	0.01%	0.24%	0.25%	N.A.	0.25%
Schwab 1000 Fund	0.20	0.29	0.49	0.02%	0.51
American Century–Benham GNMA	0.28	0.30	0.58	N.A.	0.58
Vanguard International Growth	0.18	0.38	0.56	0.12	0.68
Fidelity Equity-Income II	0.51	0.21	0.72	0.10	0.82
William Blair Growth Fund	0.68	0.11	0.79	0.09	0.88
Neuberger & Berman Partners	0.76	0.08	0.84	0.33	1.17
Oakmark Fund	1.00	0.18	1.18	0.08	1.26
Longleaf Partners Small Cap	1.00	0.23	1.23	0.19	1.42

[a]Brokerage costs are not reported for bond mutual funds because they are included in the price of the bonds.
Source: Morningstar No-Load Funds.

figure tells you what portion of your fund's earnings you are paying in expenses. It is derived by dividing your fund's all-in expense ratio, including operating expenses and brokerage costs, by its total return. The result is the ratio of all expenses to total return. This view of fund expenses is illustrated in Exhibit 4-7. The level of costs may surprise you. For a fund with a total return of 10 percent, costs of 1.75 percent of assets represent 17.5 percent of that return.

Of course, these cost percentages vary with the level of total return on investment. For a fund earning a 20 percent total return, expenses of 1.50 percent of assets represent 7.5 percent of that return. If the fund earns only 5 percent, expenses of 1.25 percent of assets equal 25 percent of total return. Since we assume that long-term returns for equity funds will average 10 percent, expenses are likely to range from 5 to 15 percent of total return.

Exhibit 4-7. Mutual fund costs as a percentage of return to investors.

Total Costs (expenses and brokerage) % of net assets	Total Return As Reported			
	5.0%	10.0%	15.0%	20.0%
	Total Costs % of Total Return			
2.50%	50.00%	25.00%	16.67%	12.50%
2.00	40.00	20.00	13.33	10.00
1.75	35.00	(17.50)	11.67	8.75
1.50	30.00	15.00	10.00	(7.50)
1.25	(25.00)	12.50	8.33	6.25
1.00	20.00	10.00	6.67	5.00
Likely Range →				
0.75	15.00	7.50	5.00	3.75
0.50	10.00	5.00	3.33	2.50
0.25	5.00	2.50	1.67	1.25

Formula: Total costs % of net assets/Total return = Total costs % of total return.

If you are using the services of an independent investment adviser, you may be paying an annual fee of 0.50 to 1.50 percent of assets. In that case, you should also know the total costs you are paying—for fund operating expenses, brokerage costs, and investment advice. And you want to be sure you are getting good results and good service for the costs you are incurring.

• *Expense projections.* The Securities and Exchange Commission (SEC) mandates that expense projections be presented in the prospectus of every fund. They show how much an investor would expect to pay in all forms of charges over the next 3, 5, and 10 years for each $1,000 investment made today. The calculations assume a $1,000 investment, 5 percent annual growth, and a redemption of your shares at the end of each period. This convention permits cost comparisons among funds for an entire ownership cycle—from initial purchase to liquidation of your position. Morningstar reports the projected costs and indicates how these expense levels compare to other funds in the same category.

These costs may seem modest to you. However, over time you are more likely to have $10,000 invested in a fund rather than $1,000. Thus, it is realistic to look at costs per $10,000 of investment. The projected costs for a $10,000 investment in a select group of mutual funds are shown in Exhibit 4-8. Note the large differences in projected costs.

Exhibit 4-8. Projected mutual fund operating expenses.

Mutual Fund	Projected Costs per $10,000 Investment			Morningstar Category	Total Cost Relative to Category
	3 Years	5 Years	10 Years		
Vanguard Short-Term Corporate	$90	$150	$340	CS	Low
Schwab 1000 Fund	160	270	620	LB	Low
Vanguard International Growth	180	310	700	FS	Low
American Century–Benham GNMA	190	320	730	GI	Low
Fidelity Equity-Income II	230	410	910	LV	Low
William Blair Growth Fund	250	440	980	MG	Low
Neuberger & Berman Partners	280	480	1,070	MB	Low
Oakmark Fund	370	650	1,430	MV	Below Average
Longleaf Partners Small Cap	410	710	1,570	SV	Average

Source: Morningstar No-Load Funds.

The exhibit also indicates the level of each fund's expense projections relative to other funds in its category. The rating is based on a bell-shaped curve. The 10 percent lowest-cost funds in each category are called "low," the next 22.5 percent "below average," and the next 35 percent "average." Funds designated "above average" and "high" bring up the rear. Aim to pick funds with at least below-average costs.

The clear message is that costs should be a major consideration in your fund selection process. For a given investment category and style, it pays to find no-load funds with low turnover in the securities they own, low brokerage costs, and low management fees and other operating expenses. Finding funds with low costs is worth the effort because costs come directly out of your return. Morningstar provides the data you need, and, of course, costs are disclosed in a fund's prospectus.

EMBRACE TAX EFFICIENCY

Mutual funds do not pay taxes themselves. Instead, they distribute the interest and dividends they receive from their investments, as well as realized short- and long-term capital gains, to their shareholders in the form of dividends. As an investor, you must then pay taxes on the dividends you receive, even if you reinvest them in more shares of the same fund.

Income taxes can significantly reduce a fund's total return. For the average equity fund, they can cut returns by even more than operating costs. The impact of operating costs and taxes on the return of a typical fund is shown in Exhibit 4-9. Together they can easily reduce your fund's after-tax return to only 75 percent of its gross return. Accordingly, put at least the same level of effort into finding funds with small potential tax liabilities as you do to selecting funds with low costs.

Funds with relatively high levels of interest, dividends, and realized gains have high tax burdens. In contrast, other funds own

Exhibit 4-9. Typical impact of operating costs and taxes on investor's return.

	% of Assets	% of Gross Return	% of Total Return
Gross return	11.25%	100.00%	—
Expense ratio	1.00	8.89	—
Brokerage costs	0.25	2.22	—
All-in costs	1.25%	11.11%	—
Total return (as reported)	(10.00)	88.89	100.00%
Income taxes	1.50	13.33	15.00
Tax-adjusted return	8.50%	(75.56%)	85.00%

stocks paying small or no dividends. They do little trading and thus realize little or no capital gains. These funds have smaller tax burdens. Most of their return to investors is in the form of *increases in their net asset value,* that is, appreciation in the price per share. Such funds are "tax efficient" because investors keep a high percentage of their pretax returns. To earn the best after-tax return, you must favor funds that are tax efficient.

You should know how taxes affect each fund you are considering for your portfolio and take that information into account in your investment decisions. To help you, Morningstar includes a tax analysis section in its one-page review of each mutual fund. This section reports (1) each fund's tax-adjusted total returns for 3, 5, and 10 years, and (2) its past tax efficiency (after-tax return as a percentage of pretax return). To determine these figures, all income and short-term capital gain distributions are taxed at the maximum federal rate of 39.6 percent. Long-term capital gains are taxed at a 28 percent rate. Since all funds are treated in the same way, it does not matter whether these rates differ from yours. The higher these ratios are, the more tax efficient the fund has been. When choosing stock funds, select those with a tax efficiency of at least 85 percent, unless you are picking funds for a tax-deferred retirement account.

Other data reported in the tax analysis section of the Morningstar page, combined with some information in the historical performance section, provide insight into a fund's likely future tax efficiency:

• *Capital gains exposure.* Many funds have unrealized capital gains in the stocks they own. These gains will be realized and taxed when the appreciated securities are sold if the gains are not offset by losses. At the end of the first quarter of 1997, domestic stock mutual funds had average potential capital gains exposure of almost 16 percent of their portfolios. This exposure ranged from 7 percent for large-value funds to 24 percent for large-growth funds. The averages for small and mid-cap funds fall between these two extremes. The higher the exposure is, the higher the potential tax burden. Eventually the gains will be realized and the tax burden passed to investors. Thus, funds with lower built-in gains are preferable. Of course, the potential capital gains do not matter for funds held in tax-deferred accounts.

• *Turnover rate.* This rate is the percentage of the portfolio that is sold and replaced during a year. A high rate indicates that the fund manager engages in frequent trading. Turnover averages 86 percent for domestic stock funds, with a range from an average of about 60 percent for large- and small-value funds to about 120 for mid-cap and small-cap growth funds. Some aggressive growth funds have turnover rates of 300 to 600 percent, indicating that they hold stocks for an average of only 2 to 4 months. Index funds are at the other extreme; they do very little trading and have turnover rates of only 1 to 5 percent. The higher the rate is, the more likely that capital gains will be realized and taxed in the future.

Annual Turnover Rate		Average Holding Period (months)
300%		4
200		6
100		12
80		15
67		18
50	Target Range	24
25		48
≤10		≥120

To minimize your tax burden, seek funds with annual turnover of less than 67 percent. This rate coincides with the 18-month holding period required for the best capital gains tax treatment under the 1997 tax law. Since 100 percent turnover means that the average holding period is 12 months, and 50 percent turnover corresponds to an average holding period of 24 months, the annual turnover consistent with an 18-month holding period is 67 percent. The formula is:

Annual turnover rate = 12 months ÷ average holding period.

Since this is an average, you may want to select funds with even less annual turnover (say, 50 percent) to ensure that your fund's capital gains are all taxed at the lowest possible rate.

• *Dividend yield.* A fund's dividend yield is its current annual dividend expressed as a percentage of the fund's net asset value:

Percentage yield = Dividend ÷ share price.

The average yield for domestic stock equity funds is less than 1 percent. Large-value stock funds have the highest average yield at 1.6 percent. Many companies pay no dividends on their common stock and thus have no dividend yield. A fund portfolio composed entirely of stocks in such companies would also have no dividend yield. Since dividends are taxable, the higher the yield, the higher your tax burden will be.

The tax efficiency indicators for selected mutual funds are shown in Exhibit 4-10. The best rule to follow is to choose funds with high historical tax efficiency and low turnover rates. Additional strategies for minimizing tax burdens are discussed in Chapter 6.

Exhibit 4-10. Indicators of tax efficiency.

Mutual Fund	Past Tax Efficiency ⇩ Tax-Adjusted Return/ Pretax Return	Indicators of Future Tax Efficiency		
		Annual Turnover Rate	Potential Capital Gains	Dividend Yield
Schwab 1000 Fund	96%	2%	33%	1.3%
Vanguard International Growth	92	22	21	1.0
Longleaf Partners Small Cap	90	28	20	0.1
William Blair Growth Fund	90	43	22	0.1
Oakmark Fund	89	24	31	0.9
Fidelity Equity-Income II	85	46	24	2.1
Neuberger & Berman Partners	84	96	27	0.8
Vanguard Short-Term Corporate	62	45	−1	6.2
American Century–Benham GNMA	56	64	−4	6.8

Source: Morningstar No-Load Funds.

If your fund has a low tax burden and operating costs, it will need to earn less gross return to achieve a given level of tax-adjusted return. With a lower target for gross return, the fund may take less risk. Thus, funds with low costs may actually be less risky than their higher-cost relatives.

PAY ATTENTION TO RISK

What is risk? That is an important question to ask, but it is not so easy to answer. In this context, risk may be thought of as the likelihood that you will lose a portion of your investment or at least that your portfolio will perform below your needs or expectations. The issue for any investor or portfolio is whether this likelihood is large or small.

Every investor should develop an understanding of risk and its relationship to return. There is no such thing as a risk-free investment. Even a U.S. government bond declines in value if interest rates rise. Thus, all investments involve some degree of risk, and risk and return are closely related. If you seek to earn greater returns, you must take on higher levels of risk.

The ultimate risk for your investment portfolio would be to invest entirely in a single common stock—the classic case of putting all your eggs in one basket. In the extreme, you could either make an excellent return or lose your entire investment based on the performance of that one company.

TYPES OF RISK

Risk comes in many different sizes and flavors. One important type of risk is *market risk*—the risk that your investment will be pulled down by an overall market decline. Another is *interest rate risk*—the risk that rates will increase and thereby reduce the value of your investment. (Remember that when interest rates go up, bond prices go down, and vice versa.) The relative importance of these two types of risk depends on your time horizon. In the short term, stocks are riskier than bonds, and you should be more concerned about market risk. In the longer term, bonds are riskier than stocks, so you should be more concerned about interest rate risk. To minimize the risk of loss, investors should rely on fixed income investments to meet short-term needs (less than 5 years) and on equities to achieve longer term goals (5 years and more).

Another important risk is the risk of being too conservative. Some people try so hard to avoid market risk that they subject themselves to an unhealthy dosage of *inflation risk*—the likelihood that asset values will be ravaged by inflation. They invest with too much emphasis on capital preservation and not enough on increased value. The result is often a return on investment below the level of inflation or too low to achieve the investor's financial goals.

The nasty thing about inflation risk is that it hurts unsuspecting investors who believe their actions (e.g., investing almost exclusively in short-term fixed income securities) will preserve the value of their investments when exactly the opposite is true. In that case, their investments are more likely to decline in real value than to grow. The challenge facing all investors is to take the right degree of risk compared to investment returns—that is, to balance risk and return.

HOW TO MEASURE RISK

There is no single universally used measure of risk. Thus, Morningstar reports several measures to help gauge a fund's risk level. Unfortunately, if you are "numerically challenged," you are likely to find this important subject among the most challenging. The measures include *standard deviation, beta, R-squared,* and a proprietary measure known as the *Morningstar risk score.* Each of these has a different focus. Here's what they mean, according to Morningstar.

• *Standard deviation.* This statistic measures how much a fund has deviated from its average total return during the specified time period, usually the previous 3 years. It takes into account both increases and declines in net asset value. A high standard deviation means greater volatility in a fund's returns, and a smaller standard deviation indicates a more consistent level of returns. Standard deviation has the advantage of measuring all funds on a common yardstick against their own performance.

A fund with a standard deviation of 15 percent is more volatile than one with a 10 percent standard deviation. A fund with an average annual return of 17 percent and a standard deviation of 9 percent is preferable to a fund with the same standard deviation and a lower average return. Since the risk is the same, the fund with the higher return is the better one.

Moreover, a fund with an average return of 19 percent and a standard deviation of 11 percent is expected to earn between 8 per-

cent and 30 percent two-thirds of the time (19 percent − 11 percent
= 8 percent, and 19 percent + 11 percent = 30 percent). As an
investor, I don't take much comfort in such large ranges, but they
certainly serve as a reminder of how volatile the stock market can
be. The total returns, standard deviations, and expected performance ranges for selected mutual funds are shown in Exhibit 4-11.

Exhibit 4-11. Range of expected returns for selected mutual funds,
ranked by standard deviation.

| Equity Mutual Fund | 3-Year Results | | Range of Expectations |
	Average Return	Standard Deviation	67% of Time (+/−1 standard deviation)
Vanguard Index 500 Fund	22.20%	12.04%	10–34%
Fidelity Equity-Income II	15.55	9.64	6–25
Longleaf Partners Small Cap	20.24	10.00	10–30
Vanguard International Growth	13.09	10.70	3–24
Oakmark Fund	19.77	11.20	8–31
Schwab 1000 Fund	19.32	11.30	8–31
Neuberger & Berman Partners	20.99	13.32	7–34
William Blair Growth Fund	16.56	13.71	3–30

Source: Morningstar No-Load Funds.

• *Beta.* According to modern portfolio theory, *beta* measures
volatility relative to an established benchmark, such as the S&P 500
Index. By definition, the benchmark index has a beta of 1.00. A
fund with a beta of .86 is less volatile than the index. A fund with
a beta of 1.10 is expected to be more volatile. It should outperform
the benchmark by 10 percent when the market goes up and trail it
by 10 percent when the market declines. Thus, if you want to reduce risk, a lower beta is better for the short term.

• *R-squared (R^2).* This measure tells you what portion of a
fund's return is based on the return of a benchmark index with

which it is being compared. For example, an R-squared of 100 means that the fund exactly matched the performance of the index. If a fund's R-squared is 33, then only 33 percent of its return is attributable to the performance of the index, and the index is not a very useful benchmark for that fund. Unfortunately, if a fund's R-squared is less than .70, its beta is a less reliable predictor of volatility. If an actively managed stock fund has an R-squared of 100, you would be better off owning a fund based on the index instead.

• *Morningstar risk score.* This proprietary measure rates downside volatility (i.e., how often a fund has underperformed the risk-free yield of a 90-day Treasury bill) on the grounds that potential reductions in value are the investor's primary concern. It also pinpoints funds that consistently underperform as being riskier than others. A score greater than 1.00 indicates that the fund is riskier than the average fund in the same broad asset category. Naturally, a score less than 1.00 is less risky.

The risk measures for selected funds are shown in Exhibit 4-12. Of course, all these measures are determined by looking at the *past* performance of a fund and its manager. The implied as-

Exhibit 4-12. Mutual fund risk measures.

| | 3-Year Results | | | | |
Equity Mutual Fund	Average Return	Standard Deviation	Beta	R-Squared	Morningstar Risk Score
Vanguard Index 500 Fund	22.20%	12.04%	1.00	100	0.70
Neuberger & Berman Partners	20.99	13.32	1.01	82	0.88
Schwab 1000 Fund	19.32	11.30	0.99	98	0.73
William Blair Growth Fund	16.56	13.71	0.91	58	1.09
Oakmark Fund	19.77	11.20	0.86	81	0.64
Fidelity Equity-Income II	15.55	9.64	0.79	81	0.73
Vanguard International Growth	13.09	10.70	0.52	31	0.64
Longleaf Partners Small Cap	20.24	10.00	0.42	25	0.59

Source: Morningstar No-Load Funds.

sumption is that the past is a reasonable predictor of the future. Much research has been done to find a good predictive measure, but researchers have concluded that there are no really good predictors of future performance. If there were, we would all use them. But since we can only look at historical performance, it makes sense to begin with funds and fund managers that have performed well rather than those that have been mediocre or poor performers.

The most commonly used historical measure of risk is standard deviation. For an individual fund, its relationship to total return is often calculated or plotted on a graph. The most often cited measure of potential future volatility is a fund's beta. In developing your portfolio, you should note both measures but focus on a fund's beta—the measure that compares a fund's performance with that of a specific index, such as the S&P 500 Index.

OTHER RISK INDICATORS

The stocks of small companies are considered riskier than those of large companies. Their market shares are likely to be smaller, their earnings are more volatile, and their access to the capital markets is more limited. Equity funds with high price/ earnings (P/E) ratios involve more risk than those with low P/E ratios. The stocks they own have further to fall if their performance does not live up to expectations or there is a general market decline. The technology and health care sectors are riskier than utilities and retailing. They face greater change and competition. And foreign stocks are riskier than domestic issues. Political and economic risk is generally greater in other countries, and relative currency values can have a major impact on performance for American investors.

Thus, in addition to the measures that focus directly on risk, look at a few other key indicators to see if they are in line with appropriate standards: the P/E ratio, the relationship between the P/E ratio and 3- to 5-year earnings growth, percentage invested in technology stocks, and percentage in foreign stocks. I like these measures to indicate less risk compared to appropriate market indexes and other funds in the same investment category. Alternatively, you may be comfortable if these measures indicate a higher level of risk.

WHAT TO DO ABOUT RISK

Although you cannot eliminate risk, your investment decisions can reduce it. By selecting funds with different but complementary characteristics, you can achieve a significant degree of diversification, and diversification reduces risk.

In fact, you have already made a commitment to diversification by adopting asset allocation targets and equity components with different objectives, investment styles, or geographic focus. By continuing to follow this approach to building your portfolio, you will ensure that it is well diversified. Your funds will likely own the stocks of more than a thousand different companies. Your funds will have different objectives, styles, betas, exposure to major indexes, and industrial sectors. By making your fund selections, you will spread the risk among a large number of companies and national economies.

Calculate the weighted average beta for your portfolio to determine whether your portfolio is more or less volatile than the S&P 500 Index. To do so, multiply your investment in each fund by the fund's beta. Add up the resulting figures for all your funds, and divide that total by the total dollar amount of your investments. The result is the weighted average beta for your mutual fund portfolio. Then decide how much risk and volatility you are willing to take compared to the market as a whole and adjust your target holdings accordingly. To assume more risk, replace a fund with a smaller beta with one whose beta is larger. Your portfolio's weighted average beta will increase.

SEEK GOOD RISK-ADJUSTED RETURNS

The ultimate test of whether your investments are successful is their after-tax return on investment—in an absolute sense, compared to other investments, and relative to the degree of risk that you elect to take. The other criteria for fund selection all serve as constraints on maximizing your return. They increase the probability of an attractive return but reduce the probability of a sensational one. In other words, you give up the potential for gigantic success in order to avoid the possibility of a colossal failure. The end result is a good risk-adjusted return.

How to Measure Return on Investment

Compared to risk, return on investment is very easy to measure. There is a single measure of the benefit to an investor from owning a mutual fund. It's called *total return*, and it is used by every newspaper, magazine, and other media that report fund performance. The total return for a fund is expressed as an annual percentage (e.g., 12 percent). Newspapers and magazines often cite returns for a month, quarter, year to date, previous 12 months, and past 3, 5, or 10 years.

Consider a fund that starts a year with a net asset value per share of $50.00. During the year it pays ordinary dividends of $1.00 per share and capital gains distributions of $1.50, both of which were reinvested in fund shares. By year end, its net asset value has increased to $55.00. What was the fund's return on investment for that year? The answer is 15 percent. The formula for a mutual fund's total return and for this example is:

$$\text{Total return} = \frac{\text{Dividends} + \text{capital gains distributions} + \text{change in net asset value}}{\text{Beginning net asset value}}$$

$$= \frac{(\$1.00 + \$1.50 + \$5.00)}{\$50.00}$$

$$= 15.0\%.$$

The numerator of the fraction is the sum of a mutual fund's income dividends, short- and long-term capital gains distributions, and increase or decrease in net asset value for the period. The denominator is the fund's net asset value at the beginning of the period. When expressed in percentage terms, this ratio provides a measure of total return from all sources. It is unaffected by whether the funds pays high dividends like an income fund or racks up large, unrealized capital gains like some growth funds. Thus, it may be used with confidence to compare the performance of all funds. The after-tax return for each fund is reported on its Morningstar page under the "Tax Analysis" heading.

Seeking Return or Limiting Risk

Some people base their investment choices almost entirely on return. They pick the fund with the highest absolute return and then look at the risk level. If the risk seems too high, they evaluate other funds with high returns until they find one with a more tolerable risk level. These investors are *return seekers.* For them, return is all important, and risk is a secondary consideration.

Others are more concerned with preserving their capital. They want an attractive return, but only within an acceptable level of risk. Thus, they tend to choose their risk level first and then see what return they can achieve without additional risk. These people are *risk limiters.* If they are falling short of their financial goals, they are more likely to invest more money at the same level of risk than to assume more risk in order to reach the required return.

I believe there are many more risk limiters than return seekers. The odds are that you and most other individual investors are risk limiters. And you should be. Avoiding risk is not your goal, but limiting it is prudent for your financial circumstances and peace of mind. Thus, the performance measures for risk and return are key to your fund selection process.

Risk-Adjusted Performance Measures

Risk measures alone provide an incomplete picture. Risk is relevant only in relation to the return that may be earned, and return is relevant only to the risk taken by the investor. Morningstar uses three good measures that take both risk and return into account. The first, its proprietary star rating system, was introduced earlier in this chapter when 4- and 5-star ratings were used as a primary fund selection criteria.

• *Sharpe ratio.* The second measure is the Sharpe ratio, named after its inventor, 1990 Nobel laureate and Stanford Business School professor William F. Sharpe. Suppose a fund had a total return of 15 percent with a standard deviation of 8 percent during a time when the return on the 90-day Treasury bill was 5 percent. Its Sharpe ratio for that time period was 1.25, calculated as follows:

$$\text{Sharpe ratio} = \frac{\text{Total return} - \text{return on 90-day Treasury bill}}{\text{Standard deviation}}$$

$$= \frac{15\% - 5\%}{8\%}$$

$$= 1.25.$$

The numerator is the "excess return" that is earned by the fund, calculated as the actual return minus the risk-free return of a 90-day Treasury bill. The denominator is the standard deviation of the fund's performance over the same time period, usually 3 years. The resulting ratio typically ranges from 0.50 to 1.50 but can be as high as 2.00 or more. The higher the ratio, the better. A high ratio indicates that the return is attractive per unit of risk. As with the other measures, the Sharpe ratio should be used to compare one fund to another.

• *Category rating.* The third measure that will help you select funds with good risk-adjusted returns is the 3-year category rating provided on the Morningstar page. It takes into account both return and risk levels compared to other stock funds in the same Morningstar category. Large-value funds are compared with other large-value funds, small-growth funds with other small-growth funds, and so forth. Thus, this rating can help you pick the best funds within a fund category regardless of how well the category is performing in relation to all other funds. Using a dial-like presentation, it rates funds on a scale of 1 to 5, with 5 being the best and 1 being the worst performer within the same category. Choose funds that have ratings of 4 or 5 within their categories. The combined risk and return measures of selected funds are shown in Exhibit 4-13.

• *M-squared.* A new measure, introduced by Morgan Stanley in early 1997, provides a way to evaluate mutual fund performance and risk. This measure was dubbed *M-squared*, after its developers, Morgan Stanley investment strategist Leah Modigliani and her grandfather, 1985 Nobel laureate Franco Modigliani. It reports a fund's risk-adjusted return on investment. This measure is defined as the return that a fund would have earned if it had the same volatility as a relevant index, such as the S&P 500.

Exhibit 4-13. Combined risk and return measures.

Equity Mutual Fund	3-Year Results					
	Morningstar Scores		Return minus Risk	3-Yr Mstar Stars	Sharpe Ratio	Category Rating
	Return	Risk				
Vanguard Index 500 Fund	1.98	0.70	1.28	*****	1.78	5
Vanguard Int'l Growth	1.82	0.64	1.18	****	0.88	4
Oakmark Fund	1.63	0.64	0.99	*****	1.62	4
Schwab 1000 Fund	1.71	0.73	0.98	*****	1.56	4
Neuberger & Berman Ptrs	1.78	0.88	0.90	****	1.17	4
Longleaf Partners Sm Cap	1.33	0.59	0.74	****	1.88	5
Fidelity Equity=Income II	1.19	0.73	0.46	****	1.33	2
William Blair Growth	1.17	1.09	0.08	***	0.99	4

Note: 1.00=average Morningstar scores for return and risk.
Source: Morningstar No-Load Funds.

Suppose, for a given time period, the S&P 500 index earned 16 percent, your mutual fund earned 15 percent, and the risk-free return of the 90-day Treasury bill was 5 percent. The index clearly outperformed the fund, and you're probably disappointed. However, the fund's standard deviation was 8 percent, and the index had a standard deviation of 10 percent, indicating that it was more volatile than your fund. Did the fund perform better or worse than the index on a risk-adjusted basis? Here is the formula for M-squared and calculations for the example:

$$
\begin{aligned}
\text{M-squared} &= \text{Risk-free return} + (\text{excess return} \times \text{relative std deviation}) \\
&= 5\% + (15\% - 5\%) \times (10\% \div 8\%) \\
&= 5\% + (10\% \times 1.25) \\
&= 17.5\%.
\end{aligned}
$$

The results can be most enlightening. After adjusting the fund's volatility to equal that of the index, the fund's risk-adjusted return was 17.5 percent. On that basis, your fund outperformed the index. You took less risk than the index but earned more for the risk you took. You should be pleased. The risk-adjusted return provides a more accurate picture of relative performance than total return alone.

For some quick insight into a fund's risk-adjusted return, compare its standard deviation with that of a benchmark market index. If the fund's standard deviation is less than the index's (i.e., standard deviation of the index ÷ standard deviation of the fund is more than 1.00), the fund's risk-adjusted return will exceed its reported return. You can then calculate the risk-adjusted return and compare it with the return of the index to see if your fund performed as well as the index on a risk-adjusted basis. Consistent underperformers should be candidates for sale; they are earning too little for the risks they take.

Unlike the other risk-adjusted measures, M-squared is not reported in *Morningstar No-Load Funds,* but the data needed to calculate it are on the Morningstar page for each fund and the Performance Close-Ups page in the Summary Section. The risk-adjusted return calculations for a selected group of no-load funds are shown in Exhibit 4-14.

M-squared has the advantage of measuring performance on a percentage basis. It is easier to understand than the Sharpe ratio, and it ranks funds in exactly the same order as the Sharpe ratio. It has already been the subject of an article in *Barrons,* and it has been introduced and used by *Money* magazine in ranking mutual funds. I think this measure is a breakthrough. It will be interesting to see if it gains wide acceptance and use. Whether it does or not, you should use it to measure the performance of funds in which you are interested.

APPLY THE SELECTION CRITERIA

When a fund's after-tax return (also known as tax-adjusted return) is calculated, the impact of other criteria—basic features, all-in

Exhibit 4-14. How to calculate M-squared (risk-adjusted return).

(A) Return of 90-day Treasury Bill 5.15% Equity Mutual Fund	(1) 3-Year Average Total Return	(2) Excess Return	(3) Actual Standard Deviation	(4) Relative Standard Deviation	(5) Risk-Adjusted Return	(6) Adjusted Rank (1=High)
Source or calculation	(enter)	(1-A)	(enter)	(Index÷Fund)	(A + (2 x 4))	(observe)
Vanguard Index 500 Fund	22.20%	17.05%	12.04%	1.00	22.20%	—
Neuberger & Berman Partners	20.99	15.84	13.32	0.90	19.47	4
Longleaf Partners Small Cap	20.24	15.09	10.00	1.20	23.32	1
Oakmark Fund	19.77	14.62	11.20	1.08	20.87	2
Schwab 1000 Fund	19.32	14.17	11.30	1.07	20.25	3
William Blair Growth Fund	16.56	11.41	13.71	0.88	15.17	6
Fidelity Equity-Income II	15.55	10.40	9.64	1.25	18.14	5
Vanguard International Growth	13.09	7.94	10.70	1.13	14.08	7

Risk adjusted return= risk free return +(excess return x (standard deviation of index ÷ standard deviation of fund))

costs, tax efficiency, and risk—has already occurred. If the return is high, it would be easy to conclude that the other criteria do not matter.

However, the challenge is to select funds that will deliver outstanding returns in the *future*. Simply picking funds with the highest historical return is not good enough. You should apply the other criteria in addition to the Morningstar 4- and 5-star ratings. It is better to find a fund that performs well because it has good underlying characteristics than to select one with good performance in spite of its poor characteristics. Those with strong basic characteristics are more likely to perform well, with less volatility, in the future.

You need to screen the funds in each investment category within *Morningstar No-Load Funds*. Use the worksheet shown in Exhibit 4-15 to evaluate and select domestic stock mutual funds. The desired standards shown on the worksheet were developed by re-

Exhibit 4-15. Domestic stock fund selection criteria.

Enter data from Morningstar page

Selection Criteria	Desired Standard	Vanguard Index 500	William Blair Growth Fund (Fund 1)	(Fund 2)	(Fund 3)
Ticker symbol	for info	VFINX	WBGSX		
Load	no-load	0	None		
Morningstar category/style	same	LB / LB	MG / MG		
Stars/3-year stars	4 or 5	5 / 5	4 /(3)		
Average rating/months	≥ 3.5 / 60	3.9 / 137	(3.3)/ 137		
Features					
Discount broker/NTF?	Yes / Yes	Y-Vanguard	Yes / Yes		
Minimum Purchase/IRA	≤ 3K / 1K	3K / 1K	(5K / 2K)		
Age of fund	5+ years	21	40+		
Tenure of manager	5+ years	9+	(4+)		
Size ($ millions)	200 – 5,000	33,738	484		
Number of stocks	50 – 200	506	67		
Costs					
Expense ratio %	≤ 1.00	0.20	0.79		
Brokerage costs %	≤ 0.25	0.02	0.09		
All-in costs %	≤ 1.25	0.22	0.88		
Relative costs	Below Avg	Below Avg	Low		
Taxes					
Tax efficiency %	≥ 85	95	89.7		
Turnover rate %	< 67	5	43		
Risk					
Standard deviation	< S&P 500	12.04	(13.71)		
Beta	.80 –1.20	1.00	0.91		
R-Squared	for info	100	58		
Morningstar risk score	< 1.00	0.70	(1.09)		
P/E ratio/relative P/E	rel< 1.00	23.4 / 1.00	29.7 /(1.25)		
3-Year earnings growth	rel > 1.00	21.8 / 1.00	29.8 / 1.36		
% foreign	< 20	3.2	5.8		
% technology	< 20	12.0	16.2		
Return					
Mean return–3 years	high	22.20	16.56		
Performance quartile	1 or 2	1	2		
Morningstar return score	> 1.00	1.98	1.17		
Sharpe ratio	> 1.00	1.78	(0.99)		
Category rating	4 or 5	5	4		
M-squared (calculate)	> S&P 500	22.20	(15.17)		

(T-Bill=5.15%)

$\bigcirc$ = Does not meet desired standard.

viewing the performance of many different funds over an extended period of time. The results for the Vanguard Index 500 Fund are already filled in to show the levels achieved by a superior performer that represents the market as a whole. The results for the William Blair Growth Fund have also been filled in as an example. Enter information from the Morningstar page for each fund you are considering and see how they compare with the desired standards and with each other.

Start by entering the fund's ticker symbol, load, and Morningstar category and investment style. Though not on the form, you may want to note the volume, issue, and date of *Morningstar No-Load Funds* that you are using, along with the page number for each fund. Then add information regarding each fund's star ratings: its overall star rating, its rating for the most recent 3 years, and its average rating during the number of months it has been rated. This average star rating is a good indicator of the fund's relative risk-adjusted performance over an extended period of time.

• *Features.* The features focus on the fund's availability, indicators of tenure, and size. Thus, they indicate whether the fund is available through a discount broker and whether it may be purchased with no transaction fee (NTF). Make a note of the minimum initial purchase for a taxable and IRA account. The age of the find and the tenure of its manager ensure that you are picking a fund with a track record and that its manager has been at the helm during that time. Finally, note the dollar amount of the fund's total assets and the number of stocks and fixed income securities that it owns.

• *Costs.* Four measures will give you a good picture of the fund's cost performance: (1) the fund's expense ratio for its most recent year, found in its historical profile; (2) its annual brokerage costs, reported at the bottom of the Morningstar page; (3) the all-in costs ratio, which is the sum of the previous two ratios; and (4) its total cost (relative to category), which indicates how the fund's 3-, 5-, and 10-year expense projections compare to other funds in the same Morningstar category.

• *Taxes.* The fund's average tax efficiency over the previous 3 years is its tax-adjusted return as a percentage of its pretax return.

This measure is reported in the Tax Analysis section of the Morn-ingstar page. The turnover rate for the most recent year is found in the History section. It indicates the likelihood that a high number of transactions will result in taxable gains in the future. These two measures provide an excellent indication of past and future tax efficiency.

- *Risk.* The risk indicators are shown in the Risk Analysis sec-tion of the Morningstar page. Enter the standard deviation, beta, R-squared, and Morningstar risk score. Then enter both the actual P/E ratio and the ratio relative to that of the S&P 500. For example, if the fund's P/E ratio is 17.5 and the S&P P/E ratio is 19.0, the relative P/E ratio is 0.92 (17.5 ÷ 19.0 = 0.92). The 3-year earnings growth of the companies owned by the fund—the actual growth rate and the growth relative to the S&P 500—should be entered next. Finally, the percentage of the fund invested in foreign stocks and in the volatile technology sector indicates whether the fund has emphasized these higher-risk segments.

- *Return.* The return measures indicate both the actual and relative total return over the previous 3 years. The performance quartile reported on the Morningstar page is for the most recent year. The Morningstar return score indicates the return relative to all domestic equity funds. The Sharpe ratio and the category rating provide insight into the risk-related return. They are found in the Risk Analysis section of the Morningstar page. You must calculate M-squared, the last measure on the page, using the fund's total return, standard deviation, and the risk-free return of the 90-day Treasury bill over the past 3 years. The return for the 90-day Trea-sury bill is found on the Performance Close-up page in the Sum-mary Section of each issue of *Morningstar No-Load Funds.* How to calculate it is shown in Exhibit 4-13.

After you have completed entering the information for several funds that you wish to consider, circle those measures that do not meet the desired standard. A purely mechanical application of the criteria is inappropriate. It may be difficult, if not impossible, to find funds that meet all of the criteria. Thus, a fund need not pass all screens to be selected for your portfolio. I suggest that you give each fund a pass or fail grade in each of the five major categories:

features, costs, taxes, risk, and return. Then choose the funds that best match the desired characteristics. As you gain experience, you may want to adjust the criteria or the desired standards to suit your own preferences and investment philosophy.

To help you pick funds, I have developed The Conover Short List of Great No-Load Mutual Funds (in Appendix B) by screening the entire fund universe against the criteria I have just described. By identifying the best 3 to 6 funds in each fund category, the list should give you a head start in selecting funds for your portfolio. In addition, my list of top-notch mutual fund families is shown in Appendix C.

5

PICKING MUTUAL FUNDS

After considering the funds' desirable features, their costs, tax efficiency, risk and return on investment, and your desired investment style, it's time to choose the specific stock, bond, and money market mutual funds that will comprise your investment portfolio. The most important choices are stock mutual funds. They likely represent the largest portion of your portfolio, and the variation in all aspects of performance among them is the greatest. The choice of bond funds is relatively straightforward, and money market funds are easy to choose if you keep in mind quality, tax status, and costs.

CHOOSE STOCK FUNDS

Based on your earlier analysis, the stock funds that you select should consist of an index fund, 3 to 5 actively managed funds with different objectives and styles, and an international fund that will provide you with exposure to many different markets around the world.

SELECTING AN INDEX FUND

The most popular market index funds offered by the different mutual fund families are the Vanguard 500 Index Fund, the Fidelity

Spartan Market Index Fund, and the Schwab 1000 Fund, which includes the second largest 500 stocks in addition to the S&P 500. Read about each of these funds in *Morningstar No-Load Funds,* and select one of them. To provide perspective, the key data on 10 domestic stock index funds are summarized in Exhibit 5-1. An impor-

Exhibit 5-1. Ten domestic equity index funds, ranked by expense ratio and turnover.

Fund	Index	Fund Size ($MM)	Number of Stocks	Date Formed	Expense Ratio	Turnover Rate	Stars
Fidelity Spartan Market Index	S&P 500	$2,970	501	3/90	0.19%	1%	4
Vanguard Index 500 Fund	S&P 500	33,738	506	8/76	0.20	5	5
Vanguard Index Growth	S&P/BARRA Growth	1,082	195	11/92	0.20	29	5
Vanguard Index Value	S&P/BARRA Value	1,161	344	11/92	0.20	29	4
Vanguard Total Stock Mkt	Wilshire 5000	3,855	2,792	4/92	0.22	3	4
Vanguard Extended Mkt	Wilshire 4500	2,167	2,139	12/87	0.25	22	3
Vanguard Small Cap Index	Russell 2000	1,734	1,568	10/60	0.25	28	2
Schwab 1000 Fund	Schwab 1000	2,106	1,007	4/91	0.49	2	4
Dreyfus Midcap Index	S&P MidCap 400	182	401	6/91	0.50	15	3
Schwab Small Cap Index	2nd 1000 Largest	237	1,101	12/93	0.59	23	2

Major Domestic Equity Stock Indexes

Index	Number of Stocks	Stocks Included in the Index
S&P 500	500	500 large stocks[a], 70% of market cap of U.S. stock market
Wilshire 4500	4,500	4,500 largest stocks, excluding S&P 500; 30% of market
Wilshire 5000	5,000	5,000 largest stocks; 100% of U.S. stock market
S&P Mid-Cap 400	400	Largest 400 stocks outside the S&P 500; market caps range from $85 million to $7 billion
Russell 1000	1,000	Largest 1,000 stocks
Russell 2000	2,000	Smallest 2,000 firms in the Russell 3000 Index
Russell 3000	3,000	Largest 3,000 stocks, as measured by market capitalization
Schwab 1000	1,000	Largest 1,000 stocks; 85% of total value of U.S. market
Schwab Small Cap	1,000	Second largest 1,000 stocks

[a]400 industrials, 20 transportation, 40 utilities, and 40 financial companies.

Source: Morningstar No-Load Funds.

tant consideration in your choice should be whether you open your brokerage account with Schwab, Fidelity, or Vanguard and which fund has the lowest expense ratio.

PICKING ACTIVELY MANAGED FUNDS

The principal goal of your actively managed funds should be to (1) earn higher returns while taking a higher level of risk, (2) reduce risk while accepting a lower return, or (3) achieve both higher returns and lower risk. Picking them is the most difficult task in developing your portfolio. The benchmark for comparing your picks should be the index fund you selected. As illustrated in Exhibit 5-2, use the style matrix to test the logic of your other individual fund selections. Enter the name of each fund selected into its appropriate style cell and the target dollar amount for each mutual fund in the right-hand column. The other column will show the actual amount that you have invested in each fund and provide a

Exhibit 5-2. Equity-style matrix showing fund selections.

(Target Total Amount = $52,000)

	Value			Blend			Growth		
Large	15% Fidelity Equity-Income II	Actual $7,500	Target $7,800	25% Schwab 1000 Fund	Actual $0	Target $13,000			
Medium	15% Oakmark Fund	Actual $0	Target $7,800	15% Neuberger & Berman Partners	Actual $4,000	Target $7,800	15% William Blair Growth Fund	Actual $6,500	Target $7,800
Small	15% Longleaf Partners Small Cap Fund	Actual $6,000	Target $7,800						

quick way for you to see your progress as you move from your current position to your target portfolio.

FINDING A REAL ESTATE FUND

Selecting a real estate mutual fund is relatively simple. There are about 50 real estate mutual funds, and the vast majority of them have sales loads of 4 to 6 percent. Only five funds with minimum initial purchase requirements of $10,000 or less (and only four with minimums of $3,000 or less) are covered in *Morningstar No-Load Funds'* real estate specialty section. Only three of them have track records of 3 years or more. The five funds are shown in Exhibit 5-3, along with some of the basic characteristics, such as the size of the fund, the number of REITs that they own, and when the fund was established. The exhibit also shows the minimum purchase required, their category ratings, and total return for a specified number of years. All the real estate mutual funds are classified as small-value funds in the equity fund–style matrix.

Exhibit 5-3. Five domestic real estate funds (ranked by fund size).

Real Estate Fund (date formed)	Fund Size ($MM)	# of REITs	Minimum Purchase	Cate- gory Rating	Years / Total Return %
Cohen & Steers Realty Shares[a] (7/91)	2,706	65	$10,000	4	5 / 19.5%
Fidelity R/E Investment Portfolio[a] (11/86)	2,190	81	2,500	5	5 / 14.6%
Vanguard Specialized REIT Index Portfolio[a] (5/96)	852	104	3,000	NR	1 / 32.1%
CGM Realty Fund (5/94)	316	24	2,500	5	3 / 23.3%
Evergreen U.S. R/E Equity Fund—Class Y (9/93)	13	38	1,000	3	3 / 22.8%

[a]Available with no transaction fee at Schwab, Fidelity, or Vanguard.
Source: Morningstar No-Load Funds, July 18, 1997.

You should read the Specialty Real Estate Overview in *Morningstar No-Load Funds* and the analyses of each fund. Then select one fund for your portfolio. Because REITs must distribute virtually all of their income to their shareholders, these funds have relatively high dividend yields and low tax efficiency. Accordingly, you should hold your real estate fund in a tax-advantaged account. When judging its performance in the future, you should compare it with the Lipper, Morgan Stanley, or Wilshire REIT Index.

CHOOSING A FOREIGN STOCK FUND

The foreign stock fund should comprise 25 percent of your equity investments. Morningstar groups funds that invest in the stocks of foreign companies into several categories. Some invest in companies from one country or region, such as Japan or Europe. Those labeled "foreign" or "international" invest in any country in the world *except* the United States. Funds called "world" or "global" may include stocks in American companies as well as those from other countries. Here are the categories along with their abbreviations:

FS	Foreign Stock	DP	Diversified Pacific Stock	EM	Diversified Emerging Mkts
WS	World Stock	JP	Japan Stock	ES	Europe Stock
IH	International Hybrid	PJ	Pacific ex Japan	LS	Latin America Stock

Since you are choosing only one international fund, your selection should be in the foreign stock category so it may invest in any country in the world outside of the United States. Morningstar covers approximately 50 foreign stock funds in *Morningstar No-Load Funds*. After you have gained experience with international funds, you may consider adding a second fund with a different size, style, or geographic focus so that it will increase your diversification. One good option for a second international fund would be a carefully selected, diversified emerging markets fund—that is, a fund that invests in the stocks of companies in developing countries, such as those in Asia and Latin America.

Begin your search for a foreign stock fund by reading the one-page Foreign Stock Overview section of *Morningstar No-Load Funds*. It lists the international stock funds with the best historical performance: the 10 with the highest total return, the 10 with the lowest risk, and the 10 with the highest overall rating. Since these lists overlap to some extent, selecting only funds that appear on these lists will narrow the field to 15 to 20 funds. A recent list of these funds is shown in Exhibit 5-4.

Exhibit 5-4. Best foreign stock funds.

Foreign Stock Funds	Best 5-Year Return	Lowest 5-Year Risk	Category Rating
Morgan Stanley Institutional Int'l	16.4%	0.63	5
Harbor International	16.2%		5
Managers International Equity	14.4%	0.52	4
Vanguard International Growth	14.1%	0.67	4
USAA International	13.9%	0.66	4
Fidelity Diversified International	13.7%	0.71	5
Hotchkiss & Wiley International	13.7%	0.68	5
Warburg Pincus International Equity	13.1%		3
Am Century–20th Century Int'l Growth	12.8%	0.69	4
Sit International Growth	12.5%		3
Babson-Stewart Ivory International		0.71	3
Schroder International		0.71	3
Scudder International		0.68	4
T. Rowe Price International Stock			4

Note: 1.00 = Average risk for equity funds
Source: Morningstar No-Load Funds, June 20, 1997

The fund you choose should have many of the same characteristics as actively managed domestic funds: no load, a 4- or 5-star rating if possible, available without transaction fees from a discount broker, low costs, tax efficient, reasonable risk, and good risk-adjusted return. Because so many new foreign funds have been launched in recent years, I believe that choosing a fund with at least a 5-year history and consistent management during that period is especially important. The oldest no-load international funds are among the offerings from the Scudder, Vanguard, and T. Rowe Price families of funds.

Another technique you may find helpful in choosing an international fund is illustrated in Exhibit 5-5. It employs the nine-cell matrix. Each fund is placed in its appropriate cell, and funds are separated into those that are available from a discount broker without any transaction fee and those on which a modest fee is charged. Most of the funds have a median market capitalization of more than $5 billion and thus fall into the large category.

You should then select a few funds for further screening

Exhibit 5-5. Investment style of best foreign stock funds.

	Value	Blend	Growth
Large	Managers International Equity[a] Hotchkiss & Wiley International[a] Morgan Stanley Institutional	Vanguard International Growth[a] Harbor International Schroder International	Sit International Growth[a] Scudder International[a] TR Price International Stock
Medium		Fidelity Diversified International[a] Warburg Pincus International Equity[a] American Century–20th Century International Growth[a] USAA International	Babson-Stewart Ivory International[a]
Small			

[a]Available with no transaction fee from Fidelity, Schwab, or Vanguard.

against the criteria shown in Exhibit 5-6. In making your choice, it is best to select a fund with a track record. You should also choose one with investments in 10 to 20 countries, and with a good distribution among European and Pacific Rim countries. The Smiths chose the Vanguard International Growth Fund for their portfolio. Its characteristics are shown in the exhibit along with the selection criteria for foreign stock funds and the desired standards for each criterion.

BUILDING AN ALL-INDEX ALTERNATIVE

If you are uncomfortable trying to pick actively managed funds that will outperform market indexes, there is an easy solution for you: Construct the domestic equity component of your portfolio entirely out of index and asset class funds. Remember that these funds are models of low-cost operations, low turnover, and tax efficiency, and history shows that they outperform the vast majority of actively managed funds. You can be confident that they will match market performance.

Designing an all-index equity portfolio is relatively easy. You simply choose from among the 14 funds shown in Exhibit 5-7. Because these funds hold companies of different sizes (as determined by market capitalization), you can use them to construct a portfolio with any mix you desire among large, meduim, and small companies. Don't forget that small companies generally offer higher returns and involve a higher level of risk than larger, well-established companies.

At one extreme, you could pick only the Vanguard Index 500 Fund, which tracks the S&P 500 Index. It holds large-value and growth stocks, and its median market capitalization is more than $25 billion, which is quite high. At the other extreme, you could focus on very small companies by choosing the DFA U.S. 9-10 Small Company Portfolio, which is offered only through financial advisers. It holds over 2,600 stocks whose size puts them in the ninth and tenth deciles of all stocks listed on the New York Stock Exchange. Its companies have market capitalizations that range from $10 million to about $200 million. Its median market capitalization

Exhibit 5-6. Foreign stock fund selection criteria.

Selection Criteria	Desired Standard	VANGUARD INTERNATIONAL GROWTH (Fund 1)	Enter data from Morningstar page (Fund 2)	(Fund 3)	(Fund 4)
Ticker symbol	for info	WWIGX			
Load	no-load	Nᴏɴᴇ			
Morningstar category/style	for info	FS / LB			
Stars/3-year stars	4 or 5	4/4			
Average rating/months	≥ 3.5 / 60	4.2/138			
Features					
Discount broker/NTF?	Yes / Yes	Yᴇs / Nᴏ			
Minimum purchase/IRA	≤ 3K / 1K	3K / 1K			
Age of fund	5+ years	15+			
Tenure of manager	5+ years	15+			
Size ($ millions)	200 – 5,000	(6,043)			
Number of stocks	50 – 200	159			
Costs					
Expense ratio %	≤ 1.50	0.56			
Brokerage costs %	≤ 0.25	0.12			
All-in costs %	≤ 1.75	0.68			
Relative costs	Below Avg	Low			
Taxes					
Tax efficiency %	≥ 80	91.9			
Turnover rate %	< 67	22			
Risk					
Standard deviation	< S&P 500	10.70			
Beta	.20 – .70	0.52			
R-squared	for info	31			
Morningstar risk score	< .90	0.64			
P/E ratio/relative P/E	rel< 1.00	28.3 /0.98			
Price/cash flow	rel < 1.00	12.0 / 0.99			
% Japan	< 20	(29)			
% technology	< 10	6.7			
Return					
Mean return–3 years	high	13.09			
Performance quartile	1 or 2	1			
Morningstar return score	> 1.00	1.82			
Sharpe ratio	> .50	0.88			
Category rating	4 or 5	4			
M-squared (calculate)	> S&P 500	(14.08)			

(T-Bɪʟʟ=5.15%)

⬭ = Does not meet desired standard.

Exhibit 5-7. Candidates for an all-index fund equity portfolio.

Domestic Fund	Number of Stocks	Cumulative Number of Stocks From Large to Small Capitalization									
		500	1,000	1,500	2,000	2,500	3,000	3,500	4,000	4,500	5,000
Largest 500 Stocks											
Vanguard Index 500 Fund	500										
Vanguard Index Growth	165										
Vanguard Index Value	335										
DFA U.S. Large Company Fund	500										
Large and mid-cap stocks											
Dreyfus Midcap Index	400										
Schwab 1000 Fund	1,000										
DFA U.S. Large Value Fund	185										
Small-cap stocks											
Schwab Small Cap Index	1,000										
Vanguard Small Cap Index	1,560										
DFA U.S. 6-10 Small Company	3,300										
DFA U.S. Small Value Fund	1,600										
DFA U.S. 9-10 Small Company	2,600										
Overall market											
Vanguard Extended Market	2,140										
Vanguard Total Stock Market	2,800										

Range of Stocks Owned by Fund

Sources: Morningstar No-Load Funds; Dimensional Fund Advisors.

Sample All-Index Fund Portfolios

Index or Asset Class Fund	% of Total	Comments
Vanguard Index 500 Fund	40%	Largest 500 domestic stocks
Vanguard Small Cap Index	40	Matches Russell 2000 index
Vanguard Index Growth	20	Achieves a large-growth tilt
Total	100%	Includes over 1,900 stocks
Schwab 1000 Fund	50%	Largest 1,000 stocks; 85% of total market capitalization
Vanguard Extended Market Fund	20	Total market except S&P 500
DFA U.S. Small Value Fund	15	Achieves value tilt among small companies
DFA U.S. 9-10 Small Company	15	Very small domestic stocks
Total	100%	Includes both largest and smallest stocks

is only $65 million, which is very low. It would be better to own both of these funds to ensure exposure to both ends of the market.

Another option is to pick Vanguard's Total Stock Market Portfolio. It holds about 2,800 stocks and tracks the Wilshire 5000 Index, which is representative of the nearly 7,000 domestic stocks. Its median market capitalization is about $10 billion. If you are very conservative, this is the one fund you should buy. It is a surrogate for the entire stock market. A better alternative to owning this one fund is to own the Vanguard 500 Index Fund and the Vanguard Extended Market Portfolio, which holds about 2,140 stocks and mimics the Wilshire 4500. Thus, it tracks the entire domestic stock market except stocks in the S&P 500. Owning both of these funds would provide you with the flexibility of being able to vary the mix between them.

In addition, by choosing different portions of the Vanguard Index Value and Vanguard Index Growth Funds, you can also tilt your holdings within the S&P 500 toward either large-value or large-growth companies, depending on your preference. Value tilts may also be achieved by choosing the DFA U.S. Large Value Fund or DFA U.S. Small Value Fund.

Combinations among the index funds are endless. In designing your all-index domestic equity portfolio, you should limit your selections to a small number of funds with relatively little overlap except to achieve desired tilts toward value or growth stocks. Two examples of all-index equity portfolios are shown in Exhibit 5-7. One other good way to achieve an all-asset-class portfolio is to work with an investment adviser approved by Dimensional Fund Advisors. You can then create a portfolio comprising entirely DFA funds and designed to provide excellent returns with low costs, low turnover, tax efficiency, and reasonable risks.

PICK BOND FUNDS

The fixed income portion of the portfolio should be invested in two, or possibly three, bond mutual funds, with general characteristics similar to those for equity funds. Thus, no-load funds with 4- or 5-star ratings, available with no transaction fee through a discount broker, are desirable. The fund managers should have track records of at least 5 years. Finally, the funds should have very low costs, which are more important for a bond fund than an equity fund because bond funds have lower total returns. An example of a Morningstar page for a bond fund is shown in Exhibit 5-8.

Morningstar categorizes domestic bond funds according to

Exhibit 5-8. Morningstar page: American Cent–Benham GNMA Fund.

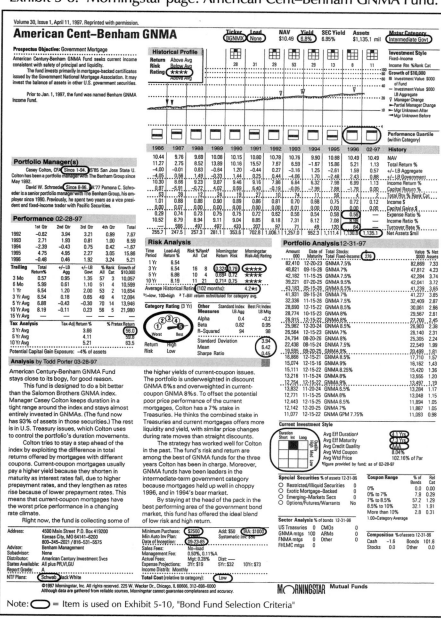

Note: ⬭ = Item is used on Exhibit 5-10, "Bond Fund Selection Criteria"

Source: Reprinted with permission of Morningstar.

their tax status, type of issuer (corporate, government, and municipal), and maturity (short-, intermediate-, and long-term). Here are
the categories along with their abbreviations:

Taxable Bond Funds		*Tax-Free Bond Funds*	
UB	Ultrashort Bond		
CS	Short-Term Bond	MS	Muni-Bond, Short-Term
CI	Intermediate-Term Bond	MI	Muni-Bond, Intermediate-Term
CL	Long-Term Bond	ML	Muni-Bond, Long-Term
CV	Convertible Bond		
HY	High-Yield Bond	MU	Multisector Bond
GS	Short-Term Govt Bond		
GI	Intermediate-Term Govt Bond	SI	Muni Single-State Intermediate
GL	Long-Term Govt Bond	SL	Muni Single-State Long

The Morningstar fixed income–style matrix will help you narrow the range of choice among bond funds. As shown in Exhibit
5-9 its two dimensions are (1) maturity or duration and (2) credit
quality. Maturity and duration are indicators of interest rate sensitivity. Both are measured in years. For example, a short-term bond
fund might have a 4-year weighted average maturity for all the
bonds it owns. Funds with shorter maturities are less risky because
their value is less sensitive to changes in interest rates, which are
difficult, if not impossible, to predict. Similarly, the higher the
credit quality, as indicated by the average bond rating, the less
chance there is that some of the bonds will default. The bond funds
you analyze for inclusion in your portfolio should be chosen for
their tax status, credit quality, and interest rate sensitivity.

• *Tax status.* If you are in at least the 28 percent federal tax
bracket (1998 taxable income of $42,350 to $102,300 on a joint return), consider tax-exempt municipal bond funds for the taxable
portion of your portfolio. They will probably provide a higher
after-tax return than taxable government or corporate bond funds
with similar maturities. If you are in a higher bracket, you should
definitely choose at least one tax-exempt fund.

Exhibit 5-9. Morningstar's fixed income–style matrix.

Risk		Maturity or Duration			Quality
		Short	Intermediate	Long	
Low	◯	Short-term High Quality	Interm-term High Quality	Long-term High Quality	High
Moderate	◖	Short-term Medium Quality	Interm-term Medium Quality	Long-term Medium Quality	Medium
High	●	Short-term Low Quality	Interm-term Low Quality	Long-term Low Quality	Low

Source: *Morningstar No-Load Funds.*

• *Credit quality.* U.S. government bonds enjoy the highest credit quality. Corporate and municipal bonds are rated by Moody's and by Standard & Poor's on a scale from AAA (the safest) to BBB (the lowest grade still considered to be of investment quality), to D, which applies to bonds in default and is the lowest rating. These ratings are shown on the Morningstar page for each fund. Bonds paying higher rates are riskier than those of the same maturity paying lower rates of interest. The quality of some municipal bond funds is enhanced by private insurance to guarantee the payment of principal at maturity. You should choose funds with at least a BBB average credit rating.

• *Interest rate sensitivity.* The value of bonds, and thus of bond funds, increases when interest rates fall and declines when interest rates rise. Why is that true? An example is warranted. Suppose you buy a perpetual bond for $1,000. It has a 6.00 percent interest rate, so it pays $60.00 in interest each year. Soon after, the market interest rate for a bond of this maturity and quality, over which you have absolutely no control, increases to 6.25 percent. In that case, the value of your bond will decline because the $60.00 in interest that the bond pays represents 6.25 percent of only $960 rather than the original $1,000 that you paid for the bond:

$$\text{Value of bond} = \text{Interest paid} \div \text{market interest rate}$$
$$= \$60.00 \div 6.25\%$$
$$= \$960.00.$$

In this example, interest rates increased from 6.00 percent to 6.25 percent, and the market value of your bond declined from $1,000 to $960, a 4 percent reduction in value. If you sell the bond today, you will get only $960 for it. Conversely, if rates had fallen, the value of your bond would have increased. To help you remember the inverse relationship between interest rates and bond prices, think of a seesaw:

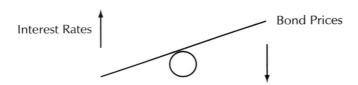

Interest rate sensitivity is an important consideration whenever fixed income investments are made. Bonds with shorter maturities are less sensitive to interest rate changes and thus less risky than those that mature later. The appropriate measure of interest rate sensitivity is the fund's duration, a measure that is somewhat linked to a bond's maturity but involves some very complex calculations. Nevertheless, it takes into account the timing of interest and principal payments and thus is a better measure of interest rate sensitivity than maturity. It is a widely used measure today. A fund with a duration of 5 years will lose 5 percent of its value if interest rates increase by 1 percentage point. Thus, the longer a bond fund's duration, the greater the risk of loss when overall interest rates rise.

When rates are low compared to historical levels, they have more room to increase than to decline further. In that case, you should choose bond funds with durations of 5 years or less, most likely from those in the short-term high quality, intermediate-term high quality, and short-term medium quality cells of the matrix. Funds with longer durations do not offer enough extra return to compensate for the additional interest rate risk.

Selection criteria for bond funds, and a worksheet for your use, are shown in Exhibit 5-10. Naturally, the criteria focus on a fund's key features, cost levels, tax efficiency, riskiness, and return. The desired standards and the data for the Vanguard Bond Index Fund Total Bond Market Portfolio provide benchmarks against which to compare the funds you choose to analyze. Data for the American Century–Benham GNMA Fund are also included on the worksheet. Measures for which an individual fund does not meet the desired standard are circled for emphasis. The specific data for each bond fund you want to analyze may be found on its Morningstar page.

SELECT A MONEY MARKET FUND

The portion of your portfolio targeted for cash equivalents should be invested in a quality money market mutual fund with check-writing privileges. Good examples are the money market offerings of Vanguard, Schwab, and Fidelity. Cash dividends and interest from other investments, except those that are automatically reinvested, should be swept into this fund every day so that they will continue to earn interest. These funds are not insured by the Federal Deposit Insurance Corporation (FDIC), but there is virtually no risk of losing your money. They invest in short-term notes (those with maturities of 60 days or less) issued by only the highest-rated government, municipal, and corporate entities. They are truly cash equivalents.

Depending on the state in which you live and your marginal income tax rate, you may want a money market fund that invests in short-term municipal bonds. For example, a California investor in the 31 percent federal tax bracket (1998 taxable joint income of $102,300 to $155,950) and an account with Charles Schwab should consider the Schwab California Tax-Exempt Money Fund. A New

Exhibit 5-10. Bond fund selection criteria.

Selection Criteria	Desired Standard	Vanguard Bond Index Total Market	AMERICAN CENTURY BENHAM GNMA (Fund 1)	(Fund 2)	(Fund 3)
Ticker symbol	for info	VBMFX	BGNMX		
Load	no-load	0	NONE		
Morningstar category/style	for info	CI / IH	GI / IH		
Stars/3-year stars	4 or 5	4 / 4	4 / 4		
Average rating/months	≥ 3.5 / 60	4.0 / 89	4.2 / 102		
Features					
Discount Broker/NTF?	Yes / Yes	Y-Vanguard	Yes / Yes		
Minimum Purchase/IRA	≤ 3K / 1K	3K / 1K	2.5K / 1K		
Age of fund	5+ years	10+	12+		
Tenure of manager	5+ years	10+	(3+ / 1+)		
Size ($ millions)	200 – 5,000	3,855	1,135		
Number of bonds	for info	801	276		
Costs					
Expense ratio %	≤ .75	0.20	0.58		
Relative costs	Below Avg	Average	Low		
Taxes					
Tax efficiency %	≥ 80	63	(56.0)		
Turnover rate %	< 67	39	64		
Risk					
Standard deviation	low	4.31	3.94		
Morningstar risk score	< 1.00	0.96	0.79		
Average duration	≤ 4.0	4.7	(4.1)		
Average maturity	≤ 8.0	8.7	7.3		
Average credit quality	BBB+	AA	AAA		
Return					
Dividend yield	for info	6.60%	6.80%		
Mean return–3 years	high	7.42%	6.42%		
Performance quartile	1 or 2	2	1		
Morningstar return score	> 1.00	0.52	(0.32)		
Sharpe ratio	≥ .50	0.67	(0.45)		
Category rating	4 or 5	4	5		

Enter data from Morningstar page

◯ = Does not meet desired standard.

Yorker in the same tax bracket should choose the Schwab NY Tax-Exempt Fund. If you don't live in a state with high tax rates, you should pick the Schwab Tax-Exempt Money Fund, which holds tax-exempt securities issued by many different states and municipal entities.

SUMMARIZE YOUR TARGET PORTFOLIO

After selecting the stock, bond, and money market mutual funds, prepare a brief summary of your target portfolio. The recommended format is shown in Exhibit 5-11. For each fund and fund

Exhibit 5-11. Summary of target portfolio.

Fund or Stock	% of Total	Target Amount	Key Fund Characteristics					
			Style[a]	Stars[b]	Costs[c]	Taxes[d]	Risk[e]	Return[f]
Schwab Money Fund	23%	$30,000	—	N.A.	0.75%	Taxable	N.A.	5.25%
American Century– Benham GNMA	10	$13,000	IH	4	0.58	56%	4.1	0.45
Vanguard Short-Term Corporate	7	10,000	SH	5	0.25	62	2.2	0.83
Total bond funds	17%	$23,000			0.44%	58%	3.3	0.61%
Schwab 1000 Fund	10	$13,000	LB	4	0.51	96	0.99	1.56
Oakmark Fund	6	7,800	MV	5	1.26	89	0.86	1.62
Fidelity Equity-Income II	6	7,800	LV	5	0.82	85	0.79	1.33
William Blair Growth Fund	6	7,800	MG	4	0.88	90	0.91	0.99
Longleaf Partners Small Cap	6	7,800	SV	5	1.42	90	0.42	1.88
Neuberger & Berman Partners	6	7,800	MB	4	1.17	84	1.01	1.17
Domestic stock funds	39%	$52,000			0.96%	90%	0.85	1.44
Vanguard International Growth Fund	15%	$20,000	LB	5	0.68	92	0.52	0.88
Total stock funds	54%	$72,000			0.88%	90%	0.76	1.32
First National Bancorp	2%	$3,000						
Heavy Metal Manufacturing	2	3,000						
Big Retail Stores	2	2,000						
Common stocks	6%	$8,000						
Total equities	60%	$80,000						
Total investment portfolio	100%	$133,000						

[a]Current style; may differ from Morningstar category.
[b]Overall star rating.
[c]All-in expense ratio = (Expense ratio + brokerage costs)/net assets.
[d]Tax efficiency percent (after-tax return/pretax return).
[e]Duration for bond funds, and beta for stock funds.
[f]Dividend yield for money market funds, and Sharpe ratio for stock and bond funds.

type it shows the percentage of the portfolio, target dollar amount, and then indicators of the key fund characteristics: investment style, star rating, all-in cost ratio, tax efficiency, level of risk, and return per unit of risk. Then inspect the summary to see if you want to change the mix of funds or fund categories in the portfolio. If necessary, make those changes.

6

MINIMIZING INCOME TAXES AFTER THE 1997 TAX LAW

I wish I could make things simple and ignore the impact of income taxes on savings and investment decisions. Taxes are complex (e.g., different tax rates and levels of deductions), and they differ for every taxpayer. Unfortunately, taxes are too important to ignore, and the new law has increased their complexity, making them even more difficult to understand.

UNDERSTAND TAX BASICS

In spite of our tax system's complexity, every investor ought to understand the basics and how taxes affect investment decisions and performance. Here's a brief update on ordinary income tax rates, capital gains taxes, and the impact of taxes on mutual fund investments.

ORDINARY INCOME TAXES

Generally, ordinary income consists of all types of earned income (e.g., salaries and wages) and net income from rental properties. It

includes interest income from bank accounts and bond investments. It also includes dividends on common stocks and mutual
fund dividends derived from *short-term capital gains,* that is, investments held for less than 1 year. On federal income tax returns,
ordinary income is taxed at 15 to 39.6 percent, as the table shows:

1998 Federal Income Tax Rates

1998 Tax Rate	Taxable Income	
	Single Taxpayers	Married Taxpayers Filing Jointly
15%	Up to $25,350	Up to $42,350
28	$25,351–61,400	$42,351–102,300
31	61,401–128,100	102,301–155,950
36	128,101–278,450	155,951–278,450
39.6	Over $278,450	Over $278,450

In addition, some states impose income taxes, which can add another 5 to 10 percent of taxable income to your already uncomfortable tax burden. To be sure that you know the size of your tax
collectors' bite, determine your combined federal and state marginal income tax rate. If your state has no income tax, your combined rate is simply the federal rate for your income bracket.

   If you live in a state with an income tax, find out what state tax
rate applies to you. To do so, obtain the state's tax rate schedules or
look at your state income tax return for last year. Since state income taxes are deductible on your federal return, you can't just
add the federal rate and the state rate together to get the combined
rate. The Smiths are subject to an 8 percent rate in California and a
28 percent federal rate. Their combined rate is 33.8 percent. The
formula for determining the combined marginal tax rate and the
calculations for the Smith family are shown in Exhibit 6-1.

   The combined marginal rate should be used in determining
after-tax returns and evaluating the relative attractiveness of taxable and tax-free investments that produce ordinary income. Because we have a graduated rate structure in which the last dollar of
earnings is taxed at a higher rate than the first dollar, your *average
rate*—the amount of taxes you pay divided by your taxable in-

Exhibit 6-1. How to calculate your combined marginal tax rate.

	Smith Family	Your Figures
A. Taxable Income, state tax return	100.0%	100.0%
B. Minus: State income tax, marginal rate (state taxes are deductible on federal tax return)	− 8.0%	
C. Equals: Taxable income, federal (A - B)	= 92.0%	
D. Times: Federal income tax, marginal rate	× 28.0%	
E. Equals: Federal income taxes (C x D)	= 25.8%	
F. Plus: State income tax rate (B)	+ 8.0%	
G. Combined marginal income tax rate (Use on exhibit 6–2, line B)	= 33.8%	

Formula: Combined marginal rate = (100% − state tax rate) × federal rate + state rate.

come—will be less than your *marginal rate.* For decision-making purposes, use your marginal rate since it is the one that will apply to income earned as a result of your investment decisions. Use the extra column on the exhibit to calculate your combined marginal rate.

CAPITAL GAINS TAXES

A *capital gain* is generated when you sell something for more than you paid for it. The gain is the selling price (less transaction costs and other selling expenses) minus the amount that you have invested in it, including your original purchase price. The total amount of your investment is known as your *cost basis.* Capital losses occur when you sell something for less than your cost basis. Mutual fund managers generate capital gains or losses when they sell stocks and bonds. Their capital gains distributions to share-holders already reflect any losses they have realized. You also real-ize capital gains or losses when you sell the mutual funds in your portfolio. With some limitations, capital losses may be offset against capital gains when determining your tax burden.

Since passage of the Taxpayer Relief Act of 1997, we now have three different rates that apply to capital gains reported on federal tax returns. The rate that applies depends on how long you have owned the asset at the time of its sale:

Holding Period	Federal Capital Gains Rate
12 months or less	Ordinary rates (15–39.6%)
12–18 months	28%
More than 18 months	20% (10% for the 15% bracket)

It is obvious that the new law favors holding investments for more than 18 months. Thus, you should look for mutual funds whose managers are more inclined to follow a buy-and-hold strat-egy than to engage in frequent trading. Moreover, you should also hold your mutual funds investments for more than 18 months whenever possible.

THE IMPACT OF TAXES

Taxes hurt. They come right out of your pocket and reduce your investment returns. The higher your tax bracket, the more pain you are likely to feel. You may also be reluctant to sell securities that will trigger payment of the capital gains tax, even at the new 20 percent rate. Thus, taxes also lock you in to investments on which you have a significant unrealized gain but are no longer perform-ing up to your expectations. Finally, they increase the amounts that you must save and invest to achieve your financial goals.

Our tax rates also provide a strong incentive for people to manage their investments in a way that will minimize their tax burdens and maximize after-tax returns. After all, it isn't how much you make; it's how much you can keep after taxes that mat-ters.

For these reasons, there is a clear trend toward emphasizing the impact of taxes and finding ways to minimize them. In 1994, the Vanguard Group launched three funds that are managed to maximize after-tax returns, and other fund families are following suit. *The Investor's Guide '98* edition of *Fortune* ranked funds according to their 5-year after-tax returns. To do so, it applied the new 20 percent long-term rate to each fund's capital gains and income distributions. The results differed from rankings on a before-tax basis, indicating that investors who focus only on pretax returns may choose the wrong funds.

Every investor's portfolio should consist of two portions: a taxable portion and a tax-advantaged portion. The characteristics of the mutual funds that you hold in each portion will have a major impact on your tax burden. For example, a fund with high income or capital gains distributions may be taxed heavily if held in a taxable account and be completely free of current taxes in a tax-deferred account. In general, tax-efficient funds should be held in taxable accounts, and funds with otherwise significant tax burdens should be held in tax-free or tax-deferred accounts.

ADOPT A STRATEGY FOR TAXABLE ACCOUNTS

Unfortunately, there are limitations regarding how much you may contribute to tax-advantaged accounts, so you will not be able to eliminate current taxes on investment income if you have a taxable investment account. Here are some rules that you should follow with regard to your taxable investments that will help minimize the damage:

• *Emphasize tax-efficient funds.* A good example of a tax-efficient fund would be an S&P 500 Index fund. It has a relatively low dividend yield, and its low turnover rate results in a low level of capital gains distributions. Any growth fund with relatively little turnover (e.g., less than 50 percent) will have little dividend income and little realized capital gains to distribute. One way to identify such a fund is to look for a growth fund with a high price per share—$40 to $70, rather than $10 to $20. Most likely, it has grown in share value rather than realizing capital gains and distributing them to shareholders.

• *Include municipal bond funds.* Your marginal tax rate may make municipal bond funds, which are tax free, an attractive investment. To permit comparisons with taxable bonds of the same maturity and credit quality, their rates are converted to *taxable-equivalent yields*. Simply put, their interest rate is adjusted to equal that of a taxable bond providing the same after-tax yield. Naturally the rate varies with the tax bracket of the individual investor. The higher the taxpayer's marginal tax rate, the higher the taxable equivalent yield, and the more attractive municipal bonds will be for that taxpayer.

The calculations for a 5 percent municipal bond under consideration by the Smith family are shown in Exhibit 6-2. Different marginal rates are used depending on whether the comparison is between a tax-free municipal bond and a fully taxable security, a U.S. Treasury issue, which is exempt from state income taxes, or a municipal bond from another state. The Smiths have a state income tax rate of 8 percent, a 28 percent federal rate, and thus a 33.8 percent combined marginal rate.

The taxable equivalent yield of the fund they are considering is 7.55 percent. Thus, they are indifferent between a 5 percent municipal bond and a fully taxable bond yielding 7.55 percent. If they can find a taxable bond yielding more than 7.55 percent, they should buy it; otherwise, the 5 percent municipal bond provides a higher after-tax return.

If you buy municipal bond funds, you must hold them in the taxable portion of your portfolio. These funds are already tax exempt and should not be put in an account with tax-advantaged status. To do so would be like wearing both a belt and suspenders to hold up your pants. A tax-advantaged account is redundant for municipal bond funds.

• *Reinvest interest and dividends.* You must follow this rule in the taxable part of your portfolio to get the benefit of compounding and maximize portfolio growth over the years. Unfortunately, in-

Exhibit 6-2. How to calculate taxable-equivalent yields.

		Smith Family	Your Figures
A. Tax-free yield (home state municipal bond)		<u>5.00%</u>	_____
Compare to fully taxable securities			
B. (1 − combined marginal tax rate) (1 - 33.8%) (From exhibit 6-1, line G)	÷	<u>66.2%</u>	_____
C. Taxable-equivalent yield (A ÷ B)	=	⬭ 7.55%	⬭
Compare to U.S. Treasury issues			
D. (1 − federal marginal tax rate) (1 - 28.0%)	÷	<u>72.0%</u>	_____
E. Taxable-equivalent yield (A ÷ D)	=	⬭ 6.94%	⬭
Compare to out-of-state municipals			
F. (1 − state marginal tax rate) (1 - 8.0%)	÷	<u>92.0%</u>	_____
G. Taxable-equivalent yield (A ÷ F)	=	⬭ 5.43%	⬭

Formula: Taxable-equivalent yield = Tax-free yield ÷ (1 − marginal tax rate).

come dividends and capital gains distributions are taxable whether they are reinvested or not.

- *Pay taxes out of earned income.* By doing so, the taxable part of your portfolio will grow as if it were tax exempt. You should adopt this practice and follow it as long as you can. If your investment program is successful, your taxable investment income may grow so large compared to your salary that you will be unable to continue this practice. In the meantime, it may put a strain on your cash flow, but it is very worthwhile. In future years, you will be glad you did it.

In any investment program, it is impossible to avoid all taxes. However, your fund choices can minimize the income taxes that you will have to pay on dividend income and capital gains distributions. Selecting funds that produce few dividends or realized capital gains can minimize your tax bill.

USE TAX-ADVANTAGED ACCOUNTS WISELY

The opportunity to defer or avoid taxes is a valuable one. Every investor should take advantage of it to the maximum extent possible. Unfortunately, the tax-related rules regarding contributions and withdrawals to these accounts are very complex. I will not deal with withdrawals (when they can be made and how much may be withdrawn without penalty). Rather, I will focus on the highlights of making contributions and how to manage these accounts to build wealth. You should review the retirement account materials offered by Charles Schwab, Fidelity Investments, or Vanguard and discuss these accounts with your tax adviser. Tax-advantaged accounts include IRA accounts, Keogh plan accounts, 401(k)s, and variable annuities.

IRA ACCOUNTS

The world of IRAs has become much more complex since the passage of the 1997 tax provisions. There are now two different kinds of IRAs that have to do with retirement: the traditional IRA, which has been around for years, and the new Roth IRA. Each has different eligibility requirements and tax treatment. (A third kind, the Education IRA, which is really an educational savings account, was discussed in the section on meeting college expenses. Generally it works like the Roth IRA.) Everyone who is eligible should have at least one of these two accounts. Taxpayers with earned income of at least $2,000 may make annual contributions of up to $2,000 to IRA accounts. A married couple may contribute up to $4,000 per year to an IRA, even if only one spouse has earnings.

THE TRADITIONAL IRA

There are three different kinds of traditional IRA accounts: deductible accounts, nondeductible accounts, and rollover accounts. Nondeductible accounts should be used only by people who are not eligible for either the deductible version of the traditional IRA or the Roth IRA. Rollover accounts are used for a very special purpose. Many people have several traditional IRA accounts with a small balance in each one. Whenever possible, these should be combined into a single account of each kind to make record keeping and account management simpler.

• *Deductible accounts.* Contributions are tax deductible if the taxpayer or spouse, for couples filing jointly, does not have a qualified retirement plan. If there is such a plan, deductibility depends on the taxpayer's AGI. In 1998, if the AGI on a joint return is $50,000 or less, the entire contribution is deductible. If AGI exceeds $60,000, no part of the contribution is deductible. If AGI is between $50,000 and $60,000, the IRA contribution is partially deductible on a sliding scale. The comparable AGI figures for a single taxpayer are $30,000 and $40,000. These eligibility ranges gradually increase until they reach $80,000 to $100,000 in 2007 for couples filing jointly and $50,000 to $70,000 in 2005 for single taxpayers. In addition, an individual not covered by a retirement plan may make deductible contributions even if his or her spouse is covered by a retirement plan, as long as the couple's joint AGI does not exceed $150,000. Because of the new tax law, many more people are eligible to make tax-deductible contributions.

The annual earnings in a traditional IRA account are tax deferred, regardless of the taxpayer's income. Taxes will not be due until the investor withdraws the funds at retirement. Withdrawals can start at age $59^1/_2$ and *must* start by age $70^1/_2$. At that time, withdrawals will be taxed at ordinary income rates. Penalties are generally assessed if funds are withdrawn before age $59^1/_2$ or if withdrawals are not started by age $70^1/_2$. Both traditional and Roth IRAs permit penalty-free early withdrawals for education expenses and up to $10,000 for first-time home purchases.

An annual IRA contribution of $2,000, invested at 8 percent

for 40 years (from age 25 to age 65), will grow, tax deferred, to exceed $600,000. However, since a $2,000 IRA contribution represents only 5 percent of an annual salary of $40,000 (much less than the Magic 13 Percent), it will not be sufficient by itself to build a retirement fund that will support you in your retirement years. You will need to build additional wealth in another account.

If you have teenage children or grandchildren who work during school vacations, you may want to contribute up to $2,000 to their traditional deductible IRA accounts. Your contribution will reduce or eliminate their tax liability and help teach them the benefits of saving and investing.

• *Nondeductible accounts.* Prior to the 1997 tax law, it made sense for some taxpayers to make contributions to traditional IRA accounts that were not tax deductible. Because of the tax-deferral feature, the full amount of any dividends and capital gains distributions could be reinvested each year. Thus, your investment could grow to a larger amount than if taxes were deducted and only the net amounts reinvested. Since passage of the new tax law, a nondeductible account makes sense for a much smaller group of taxpayers: those with qualified retirement plans and AGI of more than $150,000. This group is not eligible for a Roth IRA or to make deductible contributions to a traditional IRA. For those who are eligible for the Roth IRA, any new nondeductible contributions should be made to a Roth IRA, where they can grow *tax free* rather than only *tax deferred.*

• *IRA rollover accounts.* An IRA rollover account may be used to transfer a lump-sum distribution from another tax-deferred retirement account, such as a defined benefit pension or a 401(k) account with a former employer. If you make such a transfer, be sure that the funds are transferred directly to your IRA rollover account. If you take possession of the funds, you will be subject to 20 percent federal withholding. One rollover account is enough, as long as you keep track of the source of each rollover amount.

THE ROTH IRA

Contributions to the Roth IRA are not tax deductible, but all interest, dividends, and capital gains accumulate tax free if assets are held for at least 5 years. Eligibility for taxpayers with pension plans phases out starting at AGI of $150,000 for couples filing jointly and $95,000 for single taxpayers. Many more people are eligible for the Roth IRA than for the traditional IRA.

The Roth IRA automatically converts any pretax return to an after-tax return. By converting that after-tax return to a pretax equivalent in the same way that taxable equivalent yields are calculated for municipal bonds, you may get a true indication of the value of the Roth IRA. For example, a corporate bond yielding 6 percent in a Roth IRA provides the same after-tax benefit to a taxpayer in the 28 percent tax bracket as another bond yielding 8.3 percent in a taxable account. Here is the general formula and the calculations for this example:

$$
\begin{aligned}
\text{Pretax equivalent} &= \text{After-tax return} \div (100\% - \text{marginal tax rate}) \\
&= 6\% \div (100 - 28\%) \\
&= 8.3\%.
\end{aligned}
$$

Similarly, a stock fund with a total return of 15 percent held in a Roth IRA provides the same benefit to the Smith family, with its 33.8 percent combined marginal tax rate, as an investment with a 23 percent return in a taxable account.

HOW TO CHOOSE

The IRA eligibility requirements are summarized in Exhibit 6-3. Because the income eligibility requirements for the traditional IRA are less than for the Roth IRA, those eligible for the traditional IRA are automatically eligible for both types of accounts. They must choose which account(s) to use and how much of their $2,000 annual contribution to put into each type of account. Exhibit 6-4 summarizes some of the features of the two IRA accounts and shows their after-tax cost of contributions and the after-tax retirement fund accumulated after 10 years. There is no fundamental advantage of using one account over the other. However, depending on your eligibility and goals, there is a preferred choice.

Here's the way to choose. If your pension status or income level (1998 AGI on a joint return of $60,000 to $150,000) makes you

Exhibit 6-3. IRA eligibility by income level and pension status.

1998 Joint Return Income Level (AGI)	Qualified Retirement Plan	No Qualified Retirement Plan
Over $150,000	• Traditional IRA (nondeductible, tax deferred)	• Traditional IRA (deductible, tax deferred)
$50,000–$150,000	• Roth IRA (nondeductible, tax free)	• Roth IRA[a] (nondeductible, tax free) • Traditional IRA (deductible, tax deferred)
$50,000 or less	• Roth IRA[a] (nondeductible, tax free) • Traditional IRA (deductible, tax deferred)	• Roth IRA[a] (nondeductible, tax free) • Traditional IRA (deductible, tax deferred)

Note: Deductible/nondeductible = deductibility of contributions from current income; tax free = earnings accumulate free of taxes, and withdrawals are not taxed; tax deferred = earnings accumulate free of taxes, but withdrawals are taxed at ordinary rates.

[a]Preferred choice to accumulate a larger retirement fund after taxes.

eligible for the Roth IRA only, make the maximum $2,000 contribution to a Roth IRA account. If you are eligible for both IRAs, your choice is to (1) make a higher after-tax contribution to the Roth IRA today to accumulate a larger retirement fund in the future or (2) minimize your current after-tax cost by contributing to a traditional IRA today and settle for a smaller retirement fund. You could also compromise and make $1,000 contributions to both, as long as your total IRA contributions do not exceed $2,000. My choice would be to maximize the amount of your retirement fund—in other words, choose the Roth IRA.

Exhibit 6-4. Choosing between the Roth IRA and a traditional IRA for a 10-year time horizon.

Assumptions	
8.0%	Pretax total return
33.8%	Combined marginal tax rate during accumulation
33.8%	Combined marginal tax rate at withdrawal
$2,000	Annual IRA contribution per person

	Roth IRA			Traditional IRA		
Eligibility Phase-Out (AGI)[a]	1998			1998[b]		
• Couples filing jointly	$150,000–160,000			$50,000–60,000		
• Single taxpayers	$95,000–110,000			$30,000–40,000		
Pretax contribution	$3,021			$2,000		
After-tax contribution	$2,000			$1,324		

Year	After-Tax Cost of IRA Contribution	IRA Contribution	Year-End Cumulative IRA Balance[c]	After-Tax Cost of IRA Contribution	IRA Contribution	Year-End Cumulative IRA Balance[c]
1	$2,000	$2,000	$ 2,160	$1,324	$2,000	$2,160
2	2,000	2,000	4,493	1,324	2,000	4,493
3	2,000	2,000	7,012	1,324	2,000	7,012
4	2,000	2,000	9,733	1,324	2,000	9,733
5	2,000	2,000	12,672	1,324	2,000	12,672
6	2,000	2,000	15,846	1,324	2,000	15,846
7	2,000	2,000	19,273	1,324	2,000	19,273
8	2,000	2,000	22,975	1,324	2,000	22,975
9	2,000	2,000	26,973	1,324	2,000	26,973
10	2,000	2,000	**31,291**	1,324	2,000	**31,291**
Less: Income taxes			0			−10,576
After-tax retirement fund			**$31,291**			**$20,715**

[a]Contributions are generally tax deductible if the taxpayer or spouse, for couples filing jointly, does not have a pension plan. If there is a pension plan, the deductibility of the contribution phases out starting with the first dollar figure and ending with the second.

[b]Eligibility ranges increase through 2007 to AGI $80,000–100,000 for couples filing jointly and $50,000–70,000 for single taxpayers.

[c]Assumes contributions are made and invested at the beginning of each year.

Keogh Accounts

There are many similarities between Keogh accounts and traditional IRAs. Contributions are deductible in calculating AGI on federal income tax returns, and taxes on earnings are deferred until funds are withdrawn. However, Keoghs are designed for the self-employed or those with outside income in addition to their principal occupation. They are widely used by lawyers, consultants, and outside corporate directors.

Keogh plans permit the largest possible annual contributions: the lesser of $30,000 or 25 percent of compensation. If you are self-employed, you can contribute up to 20 percent of your income minus deductible self-employment taxes. To get the maximum contribution and preserve your flexibility, you should establish a money purchase plan with a 10 percent *mandatory* contribution and a profit-sharing plan with a 15 percent *discretionary* contribution. These plans have some administrative and filing requirements that can be quite extensive and may require professional assistance.

Because of the large amounts that may be contributed to these plans, they may enable you to cover all of your retirement funding needs, even if your compensation level is $120,000 to $200,000. Clearly an annual contribution of 20 or 25 percent will permit you to accumulate a sizable retirement nest egg or to play catch-up if you have been late in starting to build your retirement fund. If you qualify, you may make contributions to a Keogh plan as well as to an IRA account.

A variation on these accounts is the Simplified Employee Pension (SEP-IRA). It has the same characteristics as the profit-sharing plan but is much simpler to establish and administer. It requires no reporting. Annual contributions are discretionary up to the lesser of $30,000 or 15 percent of compensation (13.04 percent for the self-employed). A good approach is to establish a SEP-IRA with discretionary payments along with a money purchase plan with mandatory contributions.

401(k) Plans

Employers establish 401(k) plans as a benefit for their employees. Also known as *defined contribution plans,* they are rapidly taking the place of the traditional defined benefit plan in which the employee is guaranteed a set percentage of his or her compensation for life. They are often referred to as *salary-reduction plans* because, unlike Keoghs and traditional IRAs, they are not deductible on your tax return. Instead, they are omitted entirely from your compensation. If your total compensation is $50,000 and you elect to make a $5,000 contribution to your 401(k), your income on your W-2 form would be reported as $45,000. Contributions are made by payroll deduction.

Contributions to 401(k) plans are limited to a percentage of income specified by your employer, or $10,000 (in 1998), whichever is less. In addition, many employers make matching contributions. For example, an employer might contribute 50 cents or $1.00 for each dollar of employee contribution up to 5 percent of income. These amounts may vest immediately or be subject to a vesting schedule. Eligibility to participate might be immediately upon becoming an employee, or there might be a waiting period. Different employers adopt different features to their plans.

With a $10,000 maximum contribution, you should be able to fund your retirement well if your compensation is $75,000 or less. You should make contributions of at least 13 percent of your income, including your employer's matching contribution. If possible, make the entire 13 percent contribution yourself, and let your employer's contribution be an added attraction. You must do everything you can, including borrowing the money for a short time, to contribute the full amount that your employer will match. You could earn an immediate 50 to 100 percent return on your investment. It could be the highest return you'll ever earn in your life. It involves no risk, and it's tax deferred. Be sure to do it.

VARIABLE ANNUITIES

A *variable annuity* should be a good way for investors to take further advantage of tax-deferred growth. An *annuity* is a contract with a life insurance company. In the accumulation phase, periodic contributions to the annuity are used to pay for a modest amount of life insurance on the investor's life, cover administrative expenses, and purchase shares in the underlying mutual funds (also known as *subaccounts*) of the investor's choice. Over time, the principal amount of the annuity should increase in value.

Annuities are like nondeductible traditional IRAs with no eligibility requirements and higher costs. Although contributions to an annuity are not tax deductible, dividends paid by the mutual funds are reinvested and grow tax deferred until withdrawals are made at retirement after age $59^1/2$. Early withdrawals are generally subject to a 10 percent tax. The value of the annuity depends on the performance of the subaccounts that you select. They could range from aggressive growth funds to short-term bond funds. Withdrawals are taxed at ordinary rates just like other tax-deferred plans. Annuities ought to be a good way to accumulate a retirement fund for many people. Unfortunately, most variable annuities are awful products. Their costs are much too high.

Consider this example. One of the major retail brokerage firms recently took a half-page advertisement in the *Wall Street Journal* to tout its new variable annuity as "an easier way to save for retirement." The text described the power of tax deferral and a variety of investment options. It mentioned the life insurance protection that guarantees that, upon your death, your beneficiaries will receive at least your total payments into the plan. It pointed out that tax-deferred compounding builds wealth faster. So far, so good. These are indeed the benefits of a variable annuity.

The fine print, however, contains the bad news. The annuity has a 1.40 percent mortality and expense charge each year. The advertisement makes no mention of other administration charges or an annual policy fee of $30. Nor does it mention the expense ratios or brokerage costs of the underlying mutual funds. However, look at it this way: If the expense ratios equal 1.35 percent, somewhat below the average for domestic equity funds, your annual return will be reduced by 2.75 percentage points (1.40 + 1.35), a huge reduction considering that over the long term, common stocks have produced total returns of about 10 percent.

There is also a *surrender charge* of 7 percent if the contract is cashed in during the first seven years. It declines by 1 percent per year for seven years. Thus, not only is this annuity product too expensive, it also has a lock-in feature designed to keep you paying its exorbitant costs. If it did not have a surrender charge, it would likely have an up-front sales charge of at least 5 percent. No wonder that variable annuities are often criticized in the popular financial press. You should never buy an annuity with such high costs.

However, not all variable annuities are designed to enrich insurance and mutual fund companies at the expense of their clients. There are a few good variable annuity products, such as those offered directly by Vanguard, Schwab, and Fidelity, and through independent investment advisors by Dimensional Fund Advisors. The best of them have no front-end load or sales charge, no surrender charge, insurance costs of less than 0.85 percent, and total charges of less than 1.50 percent. They also have a variety of subaccounts with above-average performance. With such products, it is possible to get the benefits of a tax-deferred annuity and incur total insurance and fund costs below the average costs for equity mutual funds alone. The features of these low-cost annuities and of a typical high-cost annuity sold by a broker are shown in Exhibit 6-5. Since the TIAA-CREF annuities shown in the exhibit are available only to teachers, Vanguard's variable annuities are the best buys for individual investors.

The 1997 tax law makes variable annuities less attractive than before the law was passed. The problem is that withdrawals are taxed at ordinary-income tax rates rather than the new 20 percent capital gains rate. If you are eligible, you should first make nondeductible contributions to a Roth IRA, where they will grow tax free. Buy a variable annuity only if you still have an appetite for tax-deferred growth after making maximum contributions to all other tax-advantaged plans for which you are eligible. In that case, a low-cost variable annuity may be a good product for you if you expect to own it long enough for the tax deferral feature to overcome the additional costs. This could be as long as 20 years if you expect to remain in a high tax bracket after you retire. In many cases, you will accumulate a larger after-tax nest egg by simply buying a tax-efficient no-load mutual fund, paying the tax on any ordinary income or capital gains during the accumulation period, and then paying the lower 20 percent capital gains tax when you sell the fund (see Exhibit 6-6).

Citing the "exploding interest in variable annuities," the *Wall Street Journal* launched a weekly column, "Annuities Watch," in

Exhibit 6-5. Eight low-cost variable annuities, ranked by total annual expenses.

Sponsor (Fund Name)	Maximum Front Load	Maximum Surrender Charge	Annual Expenses (% of Assets) Insurance	Fund	Total	Annual Contract Charge
TIAA–CREF[a] (equity index)	None	None	0.23%	0.10%	0.33%	None
Vanguard Group (equity index)	None	None	0.48%	0.28%	0.76%	$25
Charles Schwab (S&P 500 portfolio)	None	None	0.85	0.35	1.20	25
Scudder (capital growth)	None	None	0.70	0.53	1.23	None
Janus Funds (growth)	None	None	0.65	0.69	1.34	30
T. Rowe Price (equity income)	None	None	0.55	0.85	1.40	None
Fidelity (equity income)	None	5%/5 years	1.00	0.56	1.56	30
Providian Life (DFA large value)[b]	None	None	0.65	1.20	1.85	30
Typical broker-sold annuity	5.0% or 7%/7 years		1.40%	1.35%	2.75%	60
Highest reported level	9.0	9.0	1.77	2.52	4.10	120

(Best Buy pointing to Vanguard Group)

[a]Teachers Insurance & Annuity Association–College Retirement Equities Fund.
[b]DFA = Dimensional Fund Advisors
Sources: Morningstar Principia for Variable Annuities/Life (November 1996); annuity prospectuses.

June 1997. The column appears every Monday along with a variable annuities page that contains unit price quotations, total return figures, expense ratios, and annuity indexes from Lipper Analytical Services. If you are considering a variable annuity, you will find this column a valuable information source.

Exhibit 6-6. Tax-efficient mutual fund vs. low-cost variable annuity, 20-year time horizon.

Assumptions

$2,000 Annual contribution after initial $5,000 investment

10.00% Pretax total return (after all fund operating expenses)
0.56% Extra cost of annuity (mortality and expense charges, administrative expenses, higher fund operating costs)
$25 Annual annuity contract charge (for account balances under $25,000)

1.50% Income return (dividends received)
2.00% Realized capital gains
6.50% Price appreciation

28.0% Marginal tax rate
20.0% Capital gains tax rate

	Contribution at Start of Year	Mutual Fund					Variable Annuity	
Year		Price Appreciation	Ordinary Income	Capital Gains	Yearly Taxes	Year-End Value	Total Return	Year-End Value
1	$ 5,000	$ 325	$ 75	$ 100	$ 41	$ 5,459	$ 447	$ 5,447
2	2,000	485	112	149	61	8,144	678	8,125
3	2,000	659	152	203	83	11,075	931	11,056
4	2,000	850	196	261	107	14,275	1,207	14,263
5	2,000	1,058	244	326	133	17,769	1,510	17,774
6	2,000	1,285	297	395	162	21,584	1,842	21,615
7	2,000	1,533	354	472	193	25,749	2,229	25,844
8	2,000	1,804	416	555	228	30,296	2,629	30,473
9	2,000	2,099	484	646	265	35,261	3,065	35,538
10	2,000	2,422	559	745	306	40,682	3,544	41,082
11	2,000	2,774	640	854	350	46,600	4,067	47,149
12	2,000	3,159	729	972	399	53,062	4,640	53,789
13	2,000	3,579	826	1,101	452	60,116	5,266	61,055
14	2,000	4,038	932	1,242	509	67,818	5,952	69,007
15	2,000	4,538	1,047	1,396	573	76,228	6,703	77,711
16	2,000	5,085	1,173	1,565	641	85,409	7,525	87,235
17	2,000	5,682	1,311	1,748	717	95,433	8,424	97,659
18	2,000	6,333	1,461	1,949	799	106,378	9,408	109,067
19	2,000	7,045	1,626	2,168	889	118,327	10,485	121,552
20	2,000	7,821	1,805	2,407	987	131,373	11,663	135,215
Total	$43,000	$62,573	$14,440	$19,253	$7,894		$92,215	

	Mutual Fund	Variable Annuity
Taxable income at withdrawal	$ 62,573	$ 92,215
Times: Tax rate	20.0%	28.0%
Income taxes at withdrawal	$ 12,515	$ 25,820
After-tax retirement fund	($118,858)	($109,395)

A SIMPLE STRATEGY FOR
TAX-ADVANTAGED ACCOUNTS

Tax-advantaged accounts enable you to benefit from a current tax exemption or deduction and tax-free or tax-deferred growth until you withdraw funds after you retire. Here are two rules you should follow to get the maximum benefit from these plans:

• *Make maximum contributions.* Put as much as you can in your IRA, 401(k), or Keogh plan account. If you employer matches any portion of your 401(k) contribution, the result will probably be the highest return on investment you will ever earn. If necessary, borrow an amount equal to your contribution to be sure that you can make one. You should also contribute the maximum allowable amount to each spouse's IRA account. If eligible, you should make nondeductible contributions to a Roth IRA. Couples that include a nonworking spouse may contribute $4,000 to their IRA accounts.

• *Hold funds with high turnover.* Funds with relatively high distributions of income and realized capital gains create large tax liabilities. By holding such funds in your IRA, 401(k), or Keogh plan account, you will avoid paying current taxes on these distributions. Instead, you will pay taxes at ordinary rates when you withdraw funds from these accounts when you are at least $59^1/_2$ years old.

Your compensation level and your employment situation may dictate that you may have only an IRA account; an IRA and a Keogh; or an IRA, a Keogh, and a 401(k) account. The rules that you should follow are: (1) make the maximum contribution to a 401(k) plan, (2) contribute all you can to a Keogh plan, and (3) contribute $2,000 per spouse to IRA accounts, preferably to a Roth IRA. After you have made the maximum contributions to these qualified plans, you might consider a low-cost variable annuity.

7

IMPLEMENTING, MONITORING, AND ADJUSTING

To benefit from the work you have already done, you must take the steps necessary to implement your portfolio, monitor its performance over time, and make adjustments to it when conditions warrant. This effort will take some discipline, but it is worth it to ensure that you are accomplishing your financial goals.

IMPLEMENT VIA DOLLAR COST AVERAGING

Once you have confirmed your portfolio mix, tax situation, risk level, and mutual fund selections, you are ready to start implementing your target portfolio.

DEVELOP AN IMPLEMENTATION PLAN

First, prepare an implementation plan in the same format shown as the Smith family's plan in Exhibit 7-1. It highlights the dollar amount of their current position in each fund and major asset cate-

Exhibit 7-1. 12-month implementation plan.

Fund/Stock	Current Portfolio (12/31/XX)	–	12-Month Target Portfolio	=	Planned Changes
Planned new investments (Exhibit 2-14) ──────────▶					($13,000)
Cash-equivalent assets	$ 37,000		$ 30,000		7,000
% of investment portfolio	31%		23%		
Fixed income assets	$ 51,000		$ 23,000		28,000
% of investment portfolio	42%		17%		
Total amount to invest in equities ──────────▶					48,000
Equities					
Schwab 1000 Fund	$ 0		$ 13,000		$13,000
Oakmark Fund	0		7,800		7,800
Fidelity Equity-Income II	7,500		7,800		300
William Blair Growth Fund	6,500		7,800		1,300
Longleaf Partners Small Cap	6,000		7,800		1,800
Neuberger & Berman Partners	4,000		7,800		3,800
Domestic funds	$24,000		$ 52,000		$28,000
Vanguard Int'l Growth	0		20,000		20,000
Total stock funds	$ 24,000		$ 72,000		$48,000
First National Bancorp	$3,000		$3,000		$ 0
Heavy Metal Manufacturing	3,000		3,000		0
Big Retail Stores	2,000		2,000		0
Common Stocks	$ 8,000		$ 8,000		$ 0
Total equities	$ 32,000		$ 80,000		48,000
% of investment portfolio	27%		60%		
Total investment portfolio	$120,000		$133,000		$13,000

gory, their target position, and the net changes required in their portfolio. To develop your own plan, enter the names of your planned and current holdings along with their dollar amounts in the first two columns. Then enter the amounts for your target portfolio in the third column, and derive the planned changes in the fourth.

One of the important features of this plan format is that it accommodates new money as well as the changes required to re-balance your portfolio to achieve a target mix. Thus, it should include the amounts you plan to save and invest out of current income in order to fund major purchases, college expenses, or your retirement fund. The plan should cover the next 12 months, and you should update it annually to reflect changes in your goals or financial situation.

There is considerable debate regarding whether an investor should invest a sizable amount all at once or gradually over time. Neither view seems to prevail. The wisdom of each method depends on whether the market increases or declines, your attitude toward risk, and your time horizon. A lump-sum investment followed by a market increase is the best possible outcome. If you invest gradually as the market increases, your gains will be less. Conversely, if the market declines after a lump-sum investment, you will have a bigger loss than if you choose to invest gradually.

Of course, nobody knows ahead of time when the market will go up and when it will go down. We only know that it will fluctuate. In that case, the gradual approach is the most conservative. It both minimizes the risk of a large loss and limits the potential for a large gain. If you have a long-term time horizon, the choice you make matters less. With these considerations in mind, choose the approach that is most comfortable for you.

My advice is for you to move from your current position to your target portfolio by investing the same amount each month over 6 to 12 months. That way, you will avoid investing all your funds at the top of the market and get the benefit of dollar cost averaging. For example, if you have $36,000 to invest, you might invest $3,000 per month for 12 months, $4,000 per month for 9 months, and so forth. By using this approach, the average cost of the funds you buy will be lower than the average share price during the period of investment. An example of how dollar cost averaging works is shown in Exhibit 7-2.

The plan format enables you to select a number of months and monthly dollar amounts for each fund so that the total amount invested each month is roughly constant. The more cautious you are, the longer the time frame you should select. Exhibit 7-3 shows the Smith family's schedule for monthly investments in stock

Exhibit 7-2. How dollar cost averaging works.

	Fixed Monthly Investment	Share Price	Shares Acquired
	$600	$10	60
	600	8	75
	600	6	100
	600	8	75
	600	12	50
Total	**$3,000**	**$44**	**360**

Average share price ($44 ÷ 5 months) = $8.80

Average share cost ($3,000 ÷ 360 shares) = $8.33

Exhibit 7-3. Schedule of planned monthly investments.

Monthly Investments by Mutual Fund[a]

			Stock Symbols					
Month	SNXFX	OAKMX	FEQTX	WBGSX	LLSCX	NPRTX	VWIGX	Total
1	$ 700		$300				$ 3,000	$ 4,000
2	900	$2,500			$ 600			4,000
3		600		$ 700	600	$ 500	1,600	4,000
4		600		600	600	500	1,700	4,000
5	1,200	600				500	1,700	4,000
6	1,300	500				500	1,700	4,000
7	1,200	500				600	1,700	4,000
8	1,200	500				600	1,700	4,000
9	1,200	500				600	1,700	4,000
10	1,800	500					1,700	4,000
11	1,800	500					1,700	4,000
12	1,700	500					1,800	4,000
	$13,000	$7,800	$300	$1,300	$1,800	$3,800	$20,000	$48,000

Totals coincide with amounts on Exhibit 7-1

[a]Amounts take into account minimum initial and additional purchases.

funds over a 12-month period. By following this schedule, they will achieve their target balances. Using this format, you can prepare a similar schedule for bond funds.

OPEN AN ASSET MANAGEMENT ACCOUNT

Once your plan is ready, open a Schwab One account at Charles Schwab or an Ultra Service account with Fidelity Investments. Both firms have offices throughout the country, and each provides 24-hour customer service, 7 days a week, to enable you to place buy and sell orders and obtain account information whenever you want. Both also offer dividend reinvestment plans at no charge, provide a single monthly statement, and have no transaction fees on over 600 no-load mutual funds. Even though having multiple accounts is cumbersome, you may also want to open an account at Vanguard to get the lowest-cost access to Vanguard's excellent equity index and bond funds.

These asset management accounts come with check-writing privileges and optional access by debit card, and they have no annual fees. To the extent possible, you should consolidate all your taxable investments into one account so that its monthly statements will provide a complete picture of your holdings. All three firms will help you accomplish the consolidation. Naturally, you will need to keep your tax-deferred investments, such as an IRA or Keogh plan, in other accounts.

MONITOR FUND PERFORMANCE

Now that your portfolio is launched, you will want to see how it is doing periodically. You can monitor the value of your funds every day in the *Wall Street Journal*, the *New York Times*, and many other newspapers. There you will see the closing net asset value and the change in net asset value for the previous business day. But the best measure of performance is *total return*. It takes into account a fund's dividend distributions as well as changes in its net asset value. Thus, it permits comparisons of the pretax returns of all types of funds.

Don't forget that you should have a long-term time horizon in mind. Daily and weekly fluctuations in value don't really matter. The appropriate time periods for reviewing the performance of your funds are year to date, most recent year or 12 months, and the latest 3 years.

Since performance is a relative concept, funds should be judged in comparison with others having the same investment style. Thus, a small-growth fund should be compared to other small-growth funds, a foreign stock fund with a large-value style to similar foreign stock funds, and a bond fund to similar bond funds with the same duration or maturity.

A fund with a total return of 25 percent, seemingly good performance, is actually a real disappointment if funds with the same investment style returned 35 percent for the same period. Similarly, a fund with a total return of 2 percent, or even *minus* 2 percent, performed very well if comparable funds or benchmark indexes reported a 10 percent loss. Of course, we would all prefer to be disappointed with the first fund than happy with the second.

One easy way to monitor your portfolio is to review your monthly statement from Schwab, Fidelity, or Vanguard to see how the value of your holdings has changed. Using that information, you ought to update your Investor's Balance Sheet semiannually or at least once a year.

I also recommend the portfolio tracking and pricing features of services like America Online and Prodigy. Update the number of shares you own after purchases, stock splits, and dividend reinvestments. The per-share values, the total value of each fund, and the value of the portfolio as a whole are automatically updated every day. Other tracking systems are available on the Internet. Once you've set them up, they make monitoring fund and portfolio performance very easy.

Several ways of monitoring the funds in your portfolio are illustrated in Exhibit 7-4. They are easy to use, and all the information required is in the Sunday edition of the *New York Times*. Here's what to do for your portfolio:

- *Rank your funds.* Begin by recording the year-to-date, 1-year, and 3-year total returns for the funds in your portfolio and the Vanguard Index 500 Fund, which is used as a surrogate for overall

Exhibit 7-4. Monitoring mutual fund portfolio performance.

Equity Fund	Cate-gory	Total Return (%)			Quartile		
		Year to Date	1 Year	3 Years	Year to Date	1 Year	3 Years
Vanguard Index 500 Fund	LB	25.2%	32.0%	27.4%	1	1	1
Neuberger & Berman Partners	MB	26.0%	37.5%	27.4%	2	1	1
Oakmark Fund	MV	25.1	33.5	24.2	1	2	2
Longleaf Partners Small Cap	SV	25.0	33.0	22.5	3	3	3
Schwab 1000 Fund	LB	24.1	30.8	26.2	2	2	1
Fidelity Equity-Income II	LV	19.2	25.0	19.8	4	4	4
William Blair Growth Fund	MG	13.9	17.1	19.8	3	3	3
Vanguard International Growth	FS	4.7	10.7	9.5	3	2	2
Simple average of 7 funds	—	19.7%	26.8%	21.3%	—	—	—

Note: Category is referred to as "type" by the *New York Times.*
Source: New York Times, November 2, 1997. Reprinted with permission.

market performance. Then rank your funds according to the total return they have achieved during the past year. This ranking tells you which funds are doing well and which are lagging. Funds with the lowest returns may bear watching.

• *Calculate portfolio performance.* To get a rough indication of how your overall portfolio is performing, calculate the simple average return of all your funds. Add up all their returns and divide the total by the number of funds that you own. Although this figure treats each fund with the same weight, it still provides a good performance estimate. If you want a more accurate figure for your portfolio and don't mind doing the arithmetic, calculate a weighted average return. In that case, the return for each fund should be weighted by your total investment in the fund. The resulting weighted average figure tells you the pretax total return for your portfolio. Of course, you really should know the after-tax and risk-adjusted returns, but the required information is only reported for 3-year periods on the Morningstar page for each fund.

• *Compare with benchmarks.* Since your funds are in different categories and have different styles, they are not intended to move in the same direction at the same rate. Thus, you should expect to see different levels of performance. To get a more accurate picture of how your funds are doing, compare their total returns with the performance of the Vanguard Index 500 Fund and the quartile figures for funds in the same category. This information is also in the Sunday edition of the *New York Times.* The quartile performance figures for each fund type (i.e., Morningstar category) are reported under the "Weekly Performance" heading in the mutual fund performance tables in the *New York Times,* along with instructions on how to interpret the data. Morningstar's 3-year performance ratings, such as "4/5," are also shown for each fund. The first figure is the fund's 3-year Morningstar rating, and the second is its *category rating,* a measure of 3-year risk-adjusted performance compared to other funds in the same category.

Three of the Smith family's funds have outperformed the Vanguard Index 500 Fund for the past year, and the Neuberger & Berman Partners Fund has at least matched the benchmark for all three time periods shown in the exhibit. The poor performance of the Vanguard International Growth Fund is the result of the downturn in Asian markets toward the end of October 1997. The quartile performance figures show that several of the Smiths' funds are lagging behind other funds in the same categories. The Smiths conclude from this information that no changes are required at present, but the funds in the third and fourth quartiles bear watching and may be candidates for sale if they do not improve their relative performance.

ADJUST PORTFOLIO HOLDINGS

When should you sell a fund? That may be the most troubling question investors face. Knowing when to buy and when to sell may be equally important for investors, but it is much harder for them to sell than to buy. Why? The decision to sell is often an admission that something did not work out as well as expected or that the earlier decision to buy was a mistake.

When you sell a fund, you will have either a gain or a loss. Clearly, a loss is a bad result, and even if you have a gain, you must pay capital gains taxes. Thus, neither result of selling is a totally pleasant one. In contrast, when you buy a fund, you are likely to have positive expectations. Therefore, buying is a positive experience, and selling is a negative one.

Some investment newsletters recommend selling specific funds, but they never seem to reveal the logic underlying their choices, and there seems to be no generally accepted rule regarding when to sell. Anyone who consistently knows when to sell is probably very rich and not disclosing his or her secret.

Nevertheless, there are some circumstances under which you should sell and readjust your portfolio. Perhaps your goals have changed, you want to reestablish your target asset mix, you have some poor-performing funds, or you may observe some events that you expect will lead to poor performance in the future. In any of these cases, you may want to sell the poor performers and reinvest in better-performing funds with the same objective and style—either those you own or other funds that meet the same high standards. When you sell, you should match your gains with any losses you may have in order to minimize your tax liability.

One trite answer to the question of when to sell is that you should buy low and sell high, something that is easy to say and hard to do. It is impossible to tell when the market will continue to grow and when it will decline. Many sage investors have sold out at a presumed peak, only to have the stock continue to climb by another 20 to 50 percent. Or they have bought when they thought the market was low, only to watch it sink even more.

Most individual investors ought not to try to "time the market"—that is, to buy or sell based on their market expectations in the short term. Their time horizons should be at least 5 years, so short-term market swings should not dictate their decisions. They should probably follow this simple rule: Buy when you have the money to invest, and sell when you need it to buy something. Nevertheless, there are some methods that investors use to determine when to sell.

CONSIDER PERFORMANCE-BASED RULES

You may want to sell your funds when they exhibit certain performance—for example:

• *Target price.* Some fund managers have firm rules about when to sell the stocks in their portfolios. For example, they sell when a stock reaches a target price that they established when they bought it. This approach takes a lot of discipline and is more appropriate for individual stocks and for active traders than for mutual fund investors.

• *Loss limits.* When a stock has declined by a specified percentage, some investors sell to minimize their losses. For example, you might choose to sell any fund whose price declines by 15 percent. Of course, you must then reinvest the proceeds in something with more appealing prospects, and you run the risk of missing at least some portion of the next market recovery. As a long-term investor, you are better off treating market declines as buying opportunities than signals to flee the market.

• *Poor performance.* If any of your funds has performed poorly relative to its peers for an extended period of time, you should sell it and buy another fund with the same style and objectives but with better expected performance. Experience shows that a fund can be a poor performer in one time period and a star in the next. If you want a definite rule, sell the fund if it has poor comparative after-tax, risk-adjusted performance for two consecutive years.

WATCH FOR TRIGGER EVENTS

Some people advocate selling when certain trigger events occur. They know from experience that such events may be leading indicators of poor performance in the future. Thus, you should put a fund on your "watch list" if any of the following events occurs:

• *Change in fund managers.* When a new manager takes over, the fund has really become a new and different fund. The manager whose performance attracted you in the first place is no longer calling the shots. Accordingly, you could adopt the rule that you should sell immediately if there are no tax consequences. If taxes will be due, it is more practical to wait and see how the new manager performs.

- *Large cash inflows.* A successful stock fund often attracts a lot of new investors. Funds can double or triple in size in very short time periods. Such increases may strain the fund manager's ability to find attractive investments, particularly in a small company fund. This event is not reason to sell immediately but should be cause to monitor the fund's performance.

- *Style drift.* There is a tendency for funds to drift into different cells in the equity-style matrix. For example, as the overall market increases, a successful fund with a medium-blend style may cross the line and become a large-blend fund. Or a fund manager may invest in stocks with different characteristics in order to bolster his or her performance. In either case, the fund's style may have changed, and it may no longer be appropriate for your portfolio. Watch its performance, and review other funds with the same characteristics to see if you should continue to hold it.

- *Sale of management company.* A new owner may presage a change in portfolio manager or in investment style, or it may impose a load on a previously no-load fund. Those who sold out at a fat price may be more interested in enjoying their new wealth than in paying attention to your interests as a shareholder. Again, see what happens for a while before taking any action.

TAKE CAPITAL GAINS TAX INTO ACCOUNT

It is especially hard to sell a fund that is currently sub-par after a number of years of good performance. If the fund is in the taxable portion of your portfolio, a sale will likely trigger payment of a capital gains tax. Unfortunately, the capital gains tax locks many investors into assets that were once good performers but are mediocre or worse today. As a nation, we have billions of dollars locked into poor investments by the capital gains tax. The new 20 percent capital gains tax rate may stimulate some investors to sell assets with embedded gains and reinvest in assets with greater return potential.

In contrast, the sale of a fund in the tax-deferred portion of your portfolio has no current tax consequences. Rather, you will be taxed at ordinary rates when you withdraw funds at retirement from your traditional IRA, 401(k), or Keogh accounts.

SELL, PAY TAXES, AND REINVEST

A tool to help you decide when to sell a fund, pay the capital gains tax, and buy another fund with a more promising future is shown in Exhibit 7-5. It enables you to compare the projected value of a fund you are considering selling, called the *old fund*, with that of

Exhibit 7-5. When to sell, pay taxes, and reinvest (per $1,000 of current value).

Example Inputs					Your Inputs
$850	Original cost of old fund (cost basis)				_____
$1,000	Current value of old fund at today's share price				_____
20%	Federal capital gains tax rate (18 months)				_____

	Continue to Hold Old Fund	Sell Old Fund, Pay Taxes, and Reinvest in New Fund at this % Total Return			Your Figures Old Fund New Fund
⟹	7.0%	9.0%	10.0%	11.0%	____ ____
Current value	$1,000	$970	$970	$970	____ ____

$1,000 − 20% × (1,000 − 850)   net of taxes and transaction fees

End of Year	Projected Value	Value of New Fund			Old Fund New Fund
1	1,070	1,057	1,067	(1,077)	____ ____
2	1,145	(1,152)	(1,174)	1,195	____ ____
3	1,225	1,256	1,291	1,327	____ ____
4	1,311	1,369	1,420	1,473	____ ____
5	1,403	1,492	1,562	1,635	____ ____
% change in 5-year value compared to old fund		6%	11%	17%	____

⟹ = Investor's choice.

◯ = First year when value of new fund exceeds projected value of old fund.

another fund you might buy as a replacement—the *new fund*. First, enter your original cost of the old fund, its current value, and your capital gains tax rate on the lines indicated. Then enter the total annual return you expect from each fund. The starting point is the current value of the old fund and the net proceeds after taxes and transaction costs for the new fund. Project the values each year in the future, to see when the value of the new fund exceeds that of the old fund. The rule is that you should sell a sub-par fund if, after paying the capital gains tax and incurring any transaction costs, the projected value of the new fund exceeds that of the old fund within 5 years. Of course, the hard part is projecting the values of both funds into the future. This form will at least provide some discipline for your thinking.

The approach illustrated in Exhibit 7-5 need not be used for funds in the tax-deferred portion of your portfolio. In that case, since there are no immediate tax consequences, you should sell and reinvest any time you find a fund with the same objective and style and a more attractive total return expectation.

If the return on the new fund is high enough, it will exceed that of the old fund after selling, paying the taxes and transaction costs, and reinvesting. The greater the difference in expected total return, the sooner a replacement fund will overcome taxes and transaction costs. In these cases, the entire balance of the old fund holdings should be sold. Selling a portion of a fund leads to holding too many funds.

8

STAYING
ASTUTE

I hope this book has shown you how to set financial goals and make the investment choices required to develop and maintain a sensible investment portfolio. If you follow the prescribed steps, you will achieve your financial goals. In particular, you will reach your chosen retirement date with an investment portfolio large enough to support you for the rest of your life. Congratulations.

PRESERVE YOUR ESTATE

You may also accumulate a nice inheritance for your heirs in the event you fail to reach your planned life expectancy of 90 years. But unless you are careful, your heirs may not inherit as much as you would like. Your estate could be subject to a marginal federal estate tax of 37 to 55 percent on amounts in excess of the federal tax exclusion—$625,000 in 1998. For example, if the Smiths had their target portfolio of $959,000 in place today, their estate would be subject to a 39 percent marginal tax rate. If they had left an estate of that size before the new tax law, it would have been hit with an estate tax bill of over $137,000 unless they had done some thoughtful estate planning.

Under the 1997 tax law, the exclusion from federal estate and gift taxes increases gradually from $600,000 in 1997 to $1 million in 2006. Here are the excluded amounts and their corresponding unified tax credits. The credits are applied against estate tax obligations to achieve the exclusions.

Year	Exclusion	Unified Credit
1997	$600,000	$192,800
1998	625,000	202,050
1999	650,000	211,300
2000–2001	675,000	220,550
2002–2003	700,000	229,800
2004	850,000	287,300
2005	950,000	326,300
2006	1,000,000	345,800

In addition, a new $1.3 million exemption (which includes the above excluded amounts) for small businesses and family farms is effective in 1998. Qualifying for this new tax break will be complicated and may require considerable assistance from lawyers and accountants.

A number of states also have inheritance taxes that can take a nasty bite out of your estate. As a practical matter, very few families will pay estate taxes in the future; however, if you live in California or New York, or anywhere else with high housing costs, you could be surprised at the size of your estate. As your portfolio grows and the net worth shown on your Investor's Balance Sheet exceeds the estate tax exclusion, you should consult an attorney who specializes in estate planning. He or she may help you avoid estate taxes entirely.

KEEP KEY MESSAGES IN MIND

Another great way to ensure the financial health of your heirs is to pass on some of the important messages and values contained in this book. Give them a copy of the book sooner rather than later. They can then build their own sensible portfolios and become astute investors themselves. Knowledge of the importance of saving and investing, and how to do it well, may very well be the best gift you can give them.

Here are some of the messages presented in earlier chapters for you to keep in mind and to pass on to others. They are summarized in Exhibit 8-1 and explained below. If you follow these rules faithfully, you and your heirs will achieve and enjoy financial security.

Exhibit 8-1. Fourteen messages to remember.

---

1. Develop a realistic plan—how much money you'll need and when you'll need it.
2. Use conservative estimates for inflation and total return.
3. Be an early starter, or catch up soon, and stick to your plan.
4. Save a constant percentage of your salary—at least the Magic 13 Percent.
5. Pay taxes on investment income out of salary.
6. Prepare and maintain your one-page Investor's Balance Sheet.
7. Set clear asset allocation targets—equities, fixed income, and cash.
8. Diversify—but hold only five to ten no-load mutual funds.
9. Choose stock funds with different styles: international, index, actively managed.
10. Do not make investments without knowing how they affect your overall portfolio.
11. Make maximum contributions to tax-advantaged plans: IRA, 401(k), Keogh.
12. Hold funds with high turnover or large dividends in tax-advantaged accounts.
13. Invest regularly, and use dollar cost averaging.
14. Track fund performance; rebalance your portfolio, and make adjustments annually.

• *Develop a realistic plan—how much money you'll need and when you'll need it.* This brief plan—no more than two pages—should be the foundation for your savings and investment activities. It should be tied to important life events, such as buying a house, sending a child to college, ensuring a financially secure retirement, or leaving an estate to your heirs. It should specify the amount and timing of your financial needs. Update it annually to reflect changes in your goals or your financial situation.

• *Use conservative estimates for inflation and total return.* Your plan will require that you make some assumptions regarding the future level of inflation and expected total return on investment. Be explicit in establishing these figures, but be conservative. It is better to choose a level of inflation that is too high and an expected return that is too low than vice versa. You can then be confident that your plans are likely to be achieved. And you may avoid the disappointment and financial hardship of discovering later that you have saved too little or been unable to achieve the total returns that you expected.

• *Be an early starter, or catch up soon, and stick to your plan.* Time and compound interest are among your greatest allies. By starting early, you can increase the likelihood that you will achieve your goals. Moreover, you will have the flexibility and time to take corrective action if your investments should get off course or events beyond your control cause a shortfall and require you to make changes in order to achieve your plans.

• *Save a constant percentage of your salary—at least the Magic 13 Percent.* Focus on saving a significant portion of your earned income or of any amount that you receive by gift or inheritance. Annual savings of 13 percent of your salary, invested at 8 percent in tax-advantaged accounts, or with taxes on investment income paid out of salary, will enable you to retire comfortably. As your income increases, adjust the amount that you save to maintain the same percentage.

• *Pay taxes on investment income out of salary.* Do this as long as you can. By doing so, your taxable portfolio will grow as if it were tax deferred. At some point in the future, if you are very successful, you will not be able to continue this practice. Your taxable investment income will grow so large relative to your salary that you will no longer be able to pay the taxes from your salary. You should hope that you will be so successful that you can no longer do this.

• *Prepare and maintain your one-page Investor's Balance Sheet.* This special way of presenting your financial statement puts emphasis on your role as an investor—a role that you should not try to avoid. Whatever your profession, your second job is to be an investor. This balance sheet enables you to have a complete picture of your wealth on only one page, plus a page of supporting data. Update it at least annually, and use it to understand your current asset mix and to track your progress in building your net worth.

• *Set clear asset allocation targets—equities, fixed income, and cash.* Asset mix is a major determinant of investment performance. Every investor should have a target asset allocation and know where he or she is toward achieving it. Test it annually to confirm your target level and make any needed adjustments.

• *Diversify—but hold only five to ten no-load mutual funds.* The way to deal with risk is to diversify so that your investment results are not too dependent on any concentration by sector, investment style, manager, or country. Thus, you want a well-diversified portfolio. A small number of funds can provide that diversification; a portfolio of five to ten funds should provide you with interests in the debt and equity securities of over 1,000 companies. There is no need to own more funds, and that number is very manageable for an individual investor.

• *Choose stock funds with different styles: international, index, actively managed.* The way to achieve diversification is to stock your portfolio with no-load mutual funds that have different characteristics and investment styles. These should include 25 percent in international stock funds and at least one market index fund (in this case the S&P 500 index fund, such as the Vanguard Index 500 Fund, the Schwab 1000 fund, or the Fidelity Spartan Market Index Fund). The three to five actively managed funds should be selected to change the expected return and risk profile of the portfolio in order to earn a higher risk-adjusted return than the core index fund.

• *Do not make investments without knowing how they affect your overall portfolio.* Many investors who have made their investments on a piecemeal basis over time end up with a portfolio that is too risk averse—too much fixed income and cash equivalents and not enough equity investments. The way to overcome that weakness that hurts your overall return is to have a plan in mind regarding the composition of your portfolio and make all investment decisions with a clear eye on their impact on the structure of the portfolio as a whole. Understand the tax-advantaged portion of your total portfolio as well as the taxable portion, and make sure that you follow appropriate strategies for each portion.

• *Make maximum contributions to tax-advantaged plans: IRA, 401(k), Keogh.* Tax-advantaged accounts enable a portfolio to grow without making withdrawals to pay taxes. Over time, the additional value of the portfolio can be very large. Thus, you must take maximum advantage of IRAs, Keogh, and especially 401(k) plans in which your employer matches your contributions. You should consider investing in a low-cost variable annuity only after taking maximum advantage of these accounts.

• *Hold funds with high turnover or large dividends in tax-advantaged accounts.* Where you hold different types of funds can have a major impact on your performance. Tax-efficient funds should be held in taxable accounts. Tax-inefficient funds—those with high turnover, high dividends, and capital gains—should be held in tax-deferred or tax-free accounts where their weaknesses are overcome by the tax-advantaged nature of the accounts themselves.

• *Invest regularly, and use dollar cost averaging.* Investing should be a way of life both while you are working and generating earned income and after your retirement. In addition, investing small amounts at regular intervals makes it less painful to divert income from spending for current enjoyment to saving for future wealth. Dollar cost averaging is a prudent way to invest.

• *Track fund performance, rebalance your portfolio and make adjustments annually.* You've got to keep score so that you know whether you are on track to achieve your financial goals. The way to proceed is to evaluate your progress at a time interval that is comfortable for you—monthly for some who are fanatic about it and annually for most other people. Since your portfolio mix will change as some funds outperform others, and some will please you and others will fail to meet your hoped for performance, you should make adjustments periodically—probably at annual intervals.

CONTINUE READING AND LEARNING

You've now got all you need to be an astute investor and to develop a sensible portfolio, but you will see lots of other material in stores, on the Internet, and on radio and television. Here are some information sources you may find helpful as you continue to monitor your mutual fund portfolio and make adjustments to it in the years ahead. It's a sign of the times that so many are on the Internet. If you do not yet have Internet access, you should get it as soon as possible. It will make your investing life much more interesting and efficient.

MAGAZINES

My evaluation of ten magazines that report on mutual fund developments and performance are contained in Appendix D. Some of them also have excellent sites on the World Wide Web:

Smart Money	http://www.smartmoney.com
Worth	http://www.worth.com

BOOKS

There are lots of books about investing. I suggest you browse through the selections offered by several booksellers with Web sites on the Internet:

AMACOM Books	http://www.amanet.org/books
Amazon Books	http://www.amazon.com
Barnes & Noble	http://www.barnesandnoble.com

NEWSLETTERS

I recommend *Morningstar Investor*, which is published monthly; an annual subscription is $79. Don't even consider subscribing to another newsletter without checking it out in *Hurlbert's Financial Digest*, a newsletter that monitors the portfolio performance claims made by investment newsletters. You can get a free copy from the PAWWS Financial Network at http://www.pawws.com.

RADIO

Listen to Bob Brinker's show called *Moneytalk*. It is on many stations throughout the country from 4 PM to 7 PM eastern time on Saturdays and Sundays. He also has a Web site at http://www.bobbrinker.com.

TELEVISION

Tune in to CNBC for its all-day coverage and analysis of and its commentary on the stock market and other business developments. Watch *Moneyline with Lou Dobbs* on CNN in the evenings. They also have Web sites:

CNBC	http://www.cnbc.com
CNNfn	http://www.cnnfn.com

THE INTERNET

Here are a dozen Web sites for you to browse. They contain plenty of information and links to lots of other useful locations.

America Online	http://www.aol.com
College Board	http://www.collegeboard.org
Fidelity	http://www.fidelity.com
Internal Revenue Service	http://www.irs.treas.gov
Intuit	http://www.intuit.com
Morningstar	http://www.morningstar.net
Motley Fool	http://www.motleyfool.com
T. Rowe Price	http://troweprice.com
Prodigy	http://www.prodigy.com
Schwab	http://www.schwab.com
Social Security Administration	http://www.ssa.gov
Vanguard	http://www.vanguard.com

As you continue to read and learn how to carry out your second job of being an investor, you will become more and more astute.

*   *   *

To get going on your investment program, order a trial subscription to *Morningstar No-Load Funds* ($45 for a 3-month trial and $175 for an annual subscription; 800/876-5005). Open a Schwab One Account, a Fidelity Ultra Service Account, or an account with Vanguard. Buy some shares in the Vanguard 500 Index Fund, Schwab 1000 Fund, or Fidelity Spartan Market Index Fund. You're on your way to becoming an astute investor. You have understanding and confidence on your side.

APPENDIX A

COMPOUND INTEREST TABLES

The arithmetic of compound interest may be used to determine the future value of an investment you own today or the present value that is equivalent to a known future amount. It is also used to convert periodic income streams or payments to lump sums, and vice versa. To make such calculations easy, compound interest tables provide the factors you need. Choose a table depending on the question you are trying to answer. Then multiply the known value by the factor in the table that corresponds to the appropriate time frame and interest rate. The result is the lump sum or periodic stream you are trying to determine. Here are some examples.

Table A-1. Inflation and Growth Factors for Projecting Values into the Future
(Future value of $1.00)

Sample Question: What will be the future value of a $2,000 investment if it grows at 8 percent per year for the next 20 years?

$$\text{Future value} = \text{Present value} \times \text{growth factor}$$
$$= \$2,000 \times 4.66 \ (8\%/20 \text{ years})$$
$$= \$9,320.$$

Sample Question: If your current salary is $8,000 per month and annual inflation is 4 percent, what must your income be in 7 years to maintain your current standard of living?

$$\text{Future salary} = \text{Present salary} \times \text{inflation factor}$$
$$= \$8{,}000 \times 1.32 \ (4\%/7 \text{ years})$$
$$= \$10{,}560.$$

Table A-2. Monthly Savings Required to Accumulate a Specific Future Amount
(Payment for a sinking fund of $1.00)

Sample Question: How much must you save and invest each month at 10 percent per year to accumulate $75,000 in 12 years?

$$\text{Monthly savings} = \text{Future value} \times \text{monthly savings factor}$$
$$= \$75{,}000 \times 0.00362 \ (10\%/12 \text{ years})$$
$$= \$271.50.$$

Tables A-3 and A-4. Future Values from Saving $1.00 per Month or Year
(Future value of $1.00 per period)

Sample Question: How much will you have in 15 years if you save $500 per month and invest it at 9 percent per year?

$$\text{Future value} = \text{Monthly savings} \times \text{future value factor}$$
$$= \$500 \times 378.41 \ (9\%/15 \text{ years})$$
$$= \$189{,}205.$$

Table A-1
Inflation and Growth Factors for Projecting Values into the Future
(Future value of $1.00)

Years	\multicolumn{8}{c}{Annual Inflation or Investment Growth Rate}
	3%	4%	5%	6%	7%	8%	9%	10%
40	3.26	4.80	7.04	10.29	14.97	21.72	31.41	45.26
39	3.17	4.62	6.70	9.70	13.99	20.12	28.82	41.14
38	3.07	4.44	6.39	9.15	13.08	18.63	26.44	37.40
37	2.99	4.27	6.08	8.64	12.22	17.25	24.25	34.00
36	2.90	4.10	5.79	8.15	11.42	15.97	22.25	30.91
35	2.81	3.95	5.52	7.69	10.68	14.79	20.41	28.10
34	2.73	3.79	5.25	7.25	9.98	13.69	18.73	25.55
33	2.65	3.65	5.00	6.84	9.33	12.68	17.18	23.23
32	2.58	3.51	4.76	6.45	8.72	11.74	15.76	21.11
31	2.50	3.37	4.54	6.09	8.15	10.87	14.46	19.19
30	2.43	3.24	4.32	5.74	7.61	10.06	13.27	17.45
29	2.36	3.12	4.12	5.42	7.11	9.32	12.17	15.86
28	2.29	3.00	3.92	5.11	6.65	8.63	11.17	14.42
27	2.22	2.88	3.73	4.82	6.21	7.99	10.25	13.11
26	2.16	2.77	3.56	4.55	5.81	7.40	9.40	11.92
25	2.09	2.67	3.39	4.29	5.43	6.85	8.62	10.83
24	2.03	2.56	3.23	4.05	5.07	6.34	7.91	9.85
23	1.97	2.46	3.07	3.82	4.74	5.87	7.26	8.95
22	1.92	2.37	2.93	3.60	4.43	5.44	6.66	8.14
21	1.86	2.28	2.79	3.40	4.14	5.03	6.11	7.40
20	1.81	2.19	2.65	3.21	3.87	4.66	5.60	6.73
19	1.75	2.11	2.53	3.03	3.62	4.32	5.14	6.12
18	1.70	2.03	2.41	2.85	3.38	4.00	4.72	5.56
17	1.65	1.95	2.29	2.69	3.16	3.70	4.33	5.05
16	1.60	1.87	2.18	2.54	2.95	3.43	3.97	4.59
15	1.56	1.80	2.08	2.40	2.76	3.17	3.64	4.18
14	1.51	1.73	1.98	2.26	2.58	2.94	3.34	3.80
13	1.47	1.67	1.89	2.13	2.41	2.72	3.07	3.45
12	1.43	1.60	1.80	2.01	2.25	2.52	2.81	3.14
11	1.38	1.54	1.71	1.90	2.10	2.33	2.58	2.85
10	1.34	1.48	1.63	1.79	1.97	2.16	2.37	2.59
9	1.30	1.42	1.55	1.69	1.84	2.00	2.17	2.36
8	1.27	1.37	1.48	1.59	1.72	1.85	1.99	2.14
7	1.23	1.32	1.41	1.50	1.61	1.71	1.83	1.95
6	1.19	1.27	1.34	1.42	1.50	1.59	1.68	1.77
5	1.16	1.22	1.28	1.34	1.40	1.47	1.54	1.61

Table A-2
Monthly Savings Required to Accumulate a Specific Future Amount
(Payment for a sinking fund of $1.00)

	Monthly Savings Required to Accumulate $1 in the Future					
Years	5%	6%	7%	8%	9%	10%
40	0.00066	0.00050	0.00038	0.00029	0.00021	0.00016
39	0.00069	0.00054	0.00041	0.00031	0.00023	0.00018
38	0.00074	0.00057	0.00044	0.00034	0.00026	0.00019
37	0.00078	0.00061	0.00048	0.00037	0.00028	0.00021
36	0.00083	0.00066	0.00051	0.00040	0.00031	0.00024
35	0.00088	0.00070	0.00056	0.00044	0.00034	0.00026
34	0.00094	0.00075	0.00060	0.00047	0.00037	0.00029
33	0.00099	0.00081	0.00065	0.00052	0.00041	0.00032
32	0.00106	0.00086	0.00070	0.00056	0.00045	0.00036
31	0.00113	0.00093	0.00076	0.00061	0.00050	0.00040
30	0.00120	0.00100	0.00082	0.00067	0.00055	0.00044
29	0.00128	0.00107	0.00089	0.00073	0.00060	0.00049
28	0.00137	0.00115	0.00096	0.00080	0.00066	0.00055
27	0.00146	0.00124	0.00104	0.00088	0.00073	0.00061
26	0.00157	0.00134	0.00114	0.00096	0.00081	0.00068
25	0.00168	0.00144	0.00123	0.00105	0.00089	0.00075
24	0.00180	0.00156	0.00134	0.00115	0.00099	0.00084
23	0.00194	0.00169	0.00147	0.00127	0.00109	0.00094
22	0.00209	0.00183	0.00160	0.00140	0.00121	0.00105
21	0.00225	0.00199	0.00175	0.00154	0.00135	0.00117
20	0.00243	0.00216	0.00192	0.00170	0.00150	0.00132
19	0.00264	0.00236	0.00211	0.00188	0.00167	0.00148
18	0.00286	0.00258	0.00232	0.00208	0.00186	0.00167
17	0.00312	0.00283	0.00256	0.00232	0.00209	0.00188
16	0.00341	0.00311	0.00284	0.00258	0.00235	0.00213
15	0.00374	0.00344	0.00315	0.00289	0.00264	0.00241
14	0.00412	0.00381	0.00352	0.00325	0.00299	0.00275
13	0.00456	0.00425	0.00395	0.00366	0.00340	0.00315
12	0.00508	0.00476	0.00445	0.00416	0.00388	0.00362
11	0.00570	0.00537	0.00505	0.00475	0.00446	0.00419
10	0.00644	0.00610	0.00578	0.00547	0.00517	0.00488
9	0.00735	0.00701	0.00667	0.00635	0.00604	0.00575
8	0.00849	0.00814	0.00780	0.00747	0.00715	0.00684
7	0.00997	0.00961	0.00926	0.00892	0.00859	0.00827
6	0.01194	0.01157	0.01122	0.01087	0.01053	0.01019
5	0.01470	0.01433	0.01397	0.01361	0.01326	0.01291

Table A-3
Future Values From Saving $1.00 per Month

Years	Future Value of $1.00 per Month Invested at . . .					
	5%	6%	7%	8%	9%	10%
40	1,526.02	1,991.49	2,624.81	3,491.01	4,681.32	6,324.08
39	1,440.06	1,864.18	2,436.30	3,211.97	4,268.41	5,713.26
38	1,358.29	1,744.26	2,260.50	2,954.31	3,890.91	5,160.34
37	1,280.50	1,631.31	2,096.54	2,716.40	3,545.78	4,659.83
36	1,206.50	1,524.92	1,943.65	2,496.72	3,230.25	4,206.76
35	1,136.09	1,424.71	1,801.05	2,293.88	2,941.78	3,796.64
34	1,069.12	1,330.32	1,668.08	2,106.59	2,678.06	3,425.39
33	1,005.40	1,241.42	1,544.06	1,933.65	2,436.95	3,089.33
32	944.78	1,157.68	1,428.41	1,773.96	2,216.51	2,785.13
31	887.12	1,078.81	1,320.56	1,626.51	2,014.99	2,509.76
30	832.26	1,004.52	1,219.97	1,490.36	1,830.74	2,260.49
29	780.07	934.54	1,126.17	1,364.64	1,662.30	2,034.85
28	730.42	868.63	1,038.69	1,248.56	1,508.30	1,830.59
27	683.19	806.55	957.11	1,141.38	1,367.51	1,645.70
26	638.26	748.07	881.02	1,042.41	1,238.80	1,478.34
25	595.51	692.99	810.07	951.03	1,121.12	1,326.83
24	554.84	641.12	743.90	866.65	1,013.54	1,189.69
23	516.16	592.25	682.19	788.73	915.18	1,065.55
22	479.35	546.23	624.65	716.79	825.26	953.17
21	444.34	502.87	570.98	650.36	743.05	851.45
20	411.03	462.04	520.93	589.02	667.89	759.37
19	379.35	423.58	474.25	532.38	599.17	676.02
18	349.20	387.35	430.72	480.09	536.35	600.56
17	320.52	353.23	390.13	431.80	478.92	532.26
16	293.24	321.09	352.27	387.21	426.41	470.44
15	267.29	290.82	316.96	346.04	378.41	414.47
14	242.60	262.30	284.04	308.02	334.52	363.81
13	219.11	235.45	253.33	272.92	294.39	317.95
12	196.76	210.15	224.69	240.51	257.71	276.44
11	175.51	186.32	197.99	210.58	224.17	238.86
10	155.28	163.88	173.08	182.95	193.51	204.84
9	136.04	142.74	149.86	157.43	165.48	174.05
8	117.74	122.83	128.20	133.87	139.86	146.18
7	100.33	104.07	108.00	112.11	116.43	120.95
6	83.76	86.41	89.16	92.03	95.01	98.11
5	68.01	69.77	71.59	73.48	75.42	77.44

Table A-4
Future Values From Saving $1.00 per Year

	Future Value of $1.00 per Year Invested at . . .					
Years	5%	6%	7%	8%	9%	10%
40	120.80	154.76	199.64	259.06	337.88	442.59
39	114.10	145.06	185.64	238.94	309.07	401.45
38	107.71	135.90	172.56	220.32	282.63	364.04
37	101.63	127.27	160.34	203.07	258.38	330.04
36	95.84	119.12	148.91	187.10	236.12	299.13
35	90.32	111.43	138.24	172.32	215.71	271.02
34	85.07	104.18	128.26	158.63	196.98	245.48
33	80.06	97.34	118.93	145.95	179.80	222.25
32	75.30	90.89	110.22	134.21	164.04	201.14
31	70.76	84.80	102.07	123.35	149.58	181.94
30	66.44	79.06	94.46	113.28	136.31	164.49
29	62.32	73.64	87.35	103.97	124.14	148.63
28	58.40	68.53	80.70	95.34	112.97	134.21
27	54.67	63.71	74.48	87.35	102.72	121.10
26	51.11	59.16	68.68	79.95	93.32	109.18
25	47.73	54.86	63.25	73.11	84.70	98.35
24	44.50	50.82	58.18	66.76	76.79	88.50
23	41.43	47.00	53.44	60.89	69.53	79.54
22	38.51	43.39	49.01	55.46	62.87	71.40
21	35.72	39.99	44.87	50.42	56.76	64.00
20	33.07	36.79	41.00	45.76	51.16	57.27
19	30.54	33.76	37.38	41.45	46.02	51.16
18	28.13	30.91	34.00	37.45	41.30	45.60
17	25.84	28.21	30.84	33.75	36.97	40.54
16	23.66	25.67	27.89	30.32	33.00	35.95
15	21.58	23.28	25.13	27.15	29.36	31.77
14	19.60	21.02	22.55	24.21	26.02	27.97
13	17.71	18.88	20.14	21.50	22.95	24.52
12	15.92	16.87	17.89	18.98	20.14	21.38
11	14.21	14.97	15.78	16.65	17.56	18.53
10	12.58	13.18	13.82	14.49	15.19	15.94
9	11.03	11.49	11.98	12.49	13.02	13.58
8	9.55	9.90	10.26	10.64	11.03	11.44
7	8.14	8.39	8.65	8.92	9.20	9.49
6	6.80	6.98	7.15	7.34	7.52	7.72
5	5.53	5.64	5.75	5.87	5.98	6.11

APPENDIX B

THE CONOVER SHORT LIST OF GREAT NO-LOAD MUTUAL FUNDS

My short list of recommended no-load mutual funds identifies some excellent funds for you to consider in developing your investment portfolio. These funds are the only ones in the universe of more than 6,000 funds that meet the specified criteria for low costs, tax efficiency, high credit quality (for bond funds), reasonable risk, and excellent return. The selected funds are presented by investment category. My goal was to identify the best 3 to 6 funds in each of 17 fund categories. The result is a list of 34 domestic equity, 6 international equity, and 27 domestic bond funds.

The list contains no sector funds, hybrid funds, long-term bond funds, or international bond funds. I think that such funds do not belong in the average investor's portfolio until the basic requirements for broad diversification have been met. Even then, they should be added cautiously because they bring an extra dimension of risk along with the potential for higher returns.

SCREENING CRITERIA

Each fund on my short list is at least 5 years old and has had the same manager for at least 3 years, and preferably for 5 years or more. Each has total assets in the $200 million to $5 billion range and, with the exception of index funds, generally holds 50 to 200 stocks or bonds. For taxable accounts, their minimum initial purchase and subsequent investment amounts are no more than $3,000 and $500, respectively.

The funds are available from Schwab, Fidelity, or Vanguard—some with no transaction fees. Not all funds are available for the same fee with each broker. Thus, you may decide to maintain accounts with two different brokers—one with Schwab or Fidelity and another with Vanguard. I have followed this practice for years, and I think it gives me access to the best funds at the lowest cost.

With few exceptions, each fund has at least a 4-star rating from Morningstar. These ratings compare each fund to its appropriate universe: all domestic equity funds, international funds, taxable bonds, or tax-free bonds. They have at least a 4 rating within their own fund category. They have no front-end loads, deferred charges, or 12b-1 fees to reduce your return on investment. To help achieve low operating costs and tax efficiency, the funds have below-average turnover rates. Their betas are generally less than that of the S&P 500 Index, indicating less volatility and risk. Their total returns for the past 3 years are above average, and their Sharpe ratios indicate that they have delivered an attractive level of return for the risks they take. Bond funds were screened to find those with high credit quality and relatively low interest rate sensitivity.

THE RESULTING LIST

The list shows the category average for the expense ratio, turnover rate, beta, Sharpe ratio, and average total return for the past 3 years. My desired standard for each category is also shown in the list. In some cases my standard is better than the average for the category, and in some cases it equals the category average. To be better than average in all criteria is quite an accomplishment.

The number of funds in each category and the number covered in *Morningstar No-Load Funds* are shown in the parentheses following each category name. Starting with a universe ranging from 647 in the large-blend category to 92 short-term municipal bond funds, the screening process narrows the choice to 3 to 6 funds in each category. Put another way, the effect is to take the 10 to 55 funds in each category within *Morningstar No-Load Funds* and screen them to find the very best 3 to 6 in each category.

The screens are mostly objective, and I performed the screening using my computer and Morningstar's *Principia Plus for Mutual Funds* software. In total, over 6,000 funds were screened against the desired standards to identify the 1 percent of funds that warrant your attention. In some cases, I supplemented the results of the objective screening with some common sense and judgment to add or delete specific funds. "Todd's Favorite Funds," my special choices for the best funds in each category, are identified with a star symbol.

ABOUT SMALL-CAP FUNDS

One of the problems in selecting funds is that they sometimes drift from one style to another. Sometimes these changes are conscious decisions by the fund manager. In other cases, they are the result of market movements. When the stock market increases for an extended period of time, as it has in the 1990s, a fund's median market capitalization is likely to increase. The result is that funds tend to drift from small to mid-cap to large. To avoid this drift, successful small-cap funds often close their books to new investors. These developments sometimes make it hard to find a good small-cap fund. Some good ones are closed to new investors, and others have drifted into mid-cap territory and are unlikely to return. If you find a good small-cap fund, buy it.

The Conover Short List follows. Since a lot of screening has already been done for you, you should feel confident that you can use the list as a starting point in selecting mutual funds for your portfolio.

THE CONOVER SHORT LIST

These no-load mutual funds are characterized by outstanding ratings relative to their peers, low costs, tax efficiency, high credit quality, reasonable risks, and excellent returns, especially for the level of risk taken. The funds within each category are ranked by their Sharpe ratios, which indicate the return per unit of risk. "Todd's Favorite Funds" within each category are identified by a star symbol to the left of the fund's name.

Domestic Equity Funds

Fund Category	Stars/ Category Rating	Current Style	Expense Ratio	Turnover Rate	Beta vs. S&P 500	Sharpe Ratio	3-Year Average Total Return
Large Value (4/25/97)							
Category average (285/31)	4/3	LV	1.37	58	0.87	1.44	17.04
Desired standard	4 or 5	LV	≤1.00	≤50	≤.90	>1.44	>17.04
Vanguard Equity-Income	4/4	LV	0.42	21	0.72	2.26	24.36
Vanguard/Windsor II[a]	4/4	LV	0.39	32	0.91	2.05	26.52
★Dodge & Cox Stock	4/4	LV	0.59	10	0.89	1.99	26.58
Large Blend (4/25/97)							
Category average (647/54)	4/3	LB	1.26	71	0.92	1.37	17.29
Desired standard	4 or 5	LB	≤1.00	≤50	≤1.00	>1.37	>17.29
TR Price G&I	4/4	LB	0.82	14	0.72	2.28	24.10
Preferred Value	4/4	LV	0.85	17	0.86	2.17	27.55
Scudder G&I	4/4	LV	0.78	27	0.80	2.13	25.11
Vanguard Index 500	4/5	LB	0.20	5	1.00	2.12	28.72
★Schwab 1000	4/4	LB	0.49	2	0.98	2.03	27.14
Large Growth (5/23/97)							
Category average (196/26)	3/3	LG	1.39	103	1.08	1.07	17.76
Desired standard	4 or 5	LG	≤1.00	<67	≤1.20	>1.07	>17.76

Note: There is a key to abbreviations used within some of the fund names on page 190.

Fund Category	(Ratings) Stars/ Category Rating	(Style) Current Style	(Costs) Expense Ratio	(Taxes) Turnover Rate	(Risk) Beta vs. S&P 500	Sharpe Ratio	(Return) 3-Year Average Total Return
Dreyfus Appreciation	4/5	LB	0.91	5	0.93	2.41	31.44
★Vanguard Index Growth	4/5	LG	0.20	29	1.06	2.14	31.85
Vanguard U.S. Growth	4/5	LG	0.43	44	0.97	2.11	29.65
Harbor Cap Appreciation[a]	4/3	LG	0.75	74	1.19	1.51	29.66
Mid-Cap Value (5/23/97)							
Category average (169/29)	3/3	MV	1.41	75	0.78	1.21	15.49
Desired standard	4 or 5	MV	≤1.25	<67	≤.90	>1.21	>15.49
Torray (10K)	5/5	LV	1.25	21	0.90	2.19	31.22
Sound Shore (5K)[a]	5/5	MV	1.15	69	0.86	2.15	27.91
Scudder Value[a]	5/5	LV	1.25	91	0.84	2.09	26.54
★Oakmark	5/4	LV	1.18	24	0.89	1.90	25.16
Mid-Cap Blend (5/23/97)							
Category average (211/33)	3/3	MB	1.42	109	0.85	1.06	15.75
Desired standard	4 or 5	MB	≤1.25	<67	≤1.00	>1.10	>15.75
Yacktman	4/5	MV	0.90	59	0.54	2.46	26.89
Evergreen G&I	4/5	MB	1.16	14	0.79	2.06	25.76
Nicholas	4/4	LB	0.74	26	0.92	1.85	24.68
★Neub & Berm Ptrs[a]	4/4	MV	0.84	96	0.98	1.84	27.18
Mid-Cap Growth (6/20/97)							
Category average (331/39)	2/3	MG	1.58	119	1.08	0.83	18.22
Desired standard	4 or 5	MG	≤1.25	<67	≤1.10	>1.10	>18.22
★TR Price Mid-Cap Gr	4/5	MB	1.04	38	0.79	1.57	25.78
TR Price New Am Gr	4/4	MB	1.01	37	0.95	1.37	24.56
William Blair Growth	4/4	MG	0.79	43	1.02	1.25	22.49

Fund Category	Ratings — Stars/ Category Rating	Style — Current Style	Costs — Expense Ratio	Taxes — Turnover Rate	Risk — Beta vs. S&P 500	Return — Sharpe Ratio	Return — 3-Year Average Total Return
Small Value (6/20/97)							
Category average (180/30)	3/3	SV	1.48	67	0.66	1.17	17.08
Desired standard	4 or 5	SV	≤1.25	≤60	≤.85	>1.17	>17.08
Longlf Ptrs Small-Cap (10K)	4/5	SB	1.23	28	0.41	2.13	24.48
Royce Premier	4/4	SV	1.25	34	0.45	1.72	18.22
★Neub & Berm Genesis[a]	4/3	SV	1.28	21	0.72	1.69	25.78
Small Blend (6/20/97)							
Category average (128/31)	2/3	SB	1.45	87	0.84	0.86	16.59
Desired standard	4 or 5	SB	≤1.25	<67	≤.90	>.86	>16.59
SSgA Small Cap[a]	4/5	SV	1.00	77	0.85	1.65	29.76
TR Price Small Cap Stock[a]	3/4	SB	1.07	31	0.62	1.49	23.44
Vanguard Index Ext Mkt	3/4	MV	0.25	22	0.90	1.38	22.36
★Nicholas Limited Edition	4/4	SB	0.86	32	0.72	1.37	23.33
Van Ind Small Cap Stock[a]	2/3	SV	0.25	28	0.86	1.17	21.22
Small Growth (7/18/97)							
Category average (231/36)	2/3	SG	1.69	124	1.01	0.86	22.56
Desired standard	4 or 5	SG	≤1.45	<67	≤1.00	>.86	>22.56
★Baron Asset	4/5	MB	1.40	19	0.94	1.41	28.32
Managers Special Equity	4/4	SB	1.43	56	0.79	1.29	24.56
Warburg Pincus Emg Gr[a]	3/4	MB	1.27	66	0.91	1.13	24.17

International Equity Funds

Fund Category	Ratings Stars/ Category Rating	Style Current Style	Costs Expense Ratio	Taxes Turnover Rate	Risk Beta vs. S&P 500	Return Sharpe Ratio	Return 3-Year Average Total Return
Foreign Stock (6/20/97)							
Category average (411/50)	3/3	—	1.69	64	0.50	0.39	8.74
Desired standard	4 or 5	—	≤1.55	<67	≤.60	>.80	>8.74
Fidelity Diversified Int'l[a]	4/5	MB	1.27	94	0.60	1.24	17.10
Managers Int'l Equity	4/4	LV	1.53	30	0.42	1.10	14.70
★Vanguard Int'l Growth	4/4	LB	0.56	22	0.56	1.06	15.58
Oakmark International	4/4	MV	1.32	42	0.46	1.03	16.52
TR Price Int'l Stock	4/4	LG	0.88	12	0.53	0.87	13.38
Scudder International	4/4	LG	1.14	45	0.56	0.80	12.68

Government Bond Funds

Fund Category	Ratings Stars/ Category Rating	Style Current Style	Costs Expense Ratio	Quality Turnover Rate	Risk Beta vs. S&P 500	Return Sharpe Ratio	3-Year Average Total Return
Short-Term Government (4/25/97)							
Category average (214/14)	3/3	SH	1.09	AAA	4.1	−0.16	4.22
Desired standard	4 or 5	SH	≤.80	AAA	≤4.1	>.50	>4.22
Sit U.S. Govt Securities[a]	5/5	IH	0.80	AAA	4.8	1.06	6.98
★Van F/I Short-Term Fed	4/4	SH	0.25	AAA	2.5	0.83	6.70
Fid Sp Ltd Mat Govt (10K)[a]	4/4	SH	0.62	AAA	4.7	0.82	7.11
Van F/I S-T US Treas	4/4	SH	0.25	AAA	2.3	0.77	6.60
Dreyfus S-Int Govt	4/3	SH	0.74	AAA	2.4	0.50	6.16
Intermediate-Term Government (4/25/97)							
Category average (349/19)	3/3	IH	1.14	AAA	8.8	0.13	5.41
Desired standard	4 or 5	IH	≤.80	AAA	≤8.8	>.50	>5.41
Vanguard F/I GNMA	4/5	IH	0.27	AAA	7.5	1.20	9.17
Fid Sp GNMA (10K)	4/5	IH	0.62	AAA	6.7	1.16	8.86
★Am Cen–Ben GNMA	4/5	IH	0.58	AAA	7.3	1.10	8.52

General Bond Funds

Fund Category	Stars/ Category Rating	Current Style	Expense Ratio	Turnover Rate	Beta vs. S&P 500	Sharpe Ratio	3-Year Average Total Return
Short-Term Bond (5/23/97)							
Category average (189/13)	3/3	SH	0.89	AA	3.3	0.33	5.58
Desired standard	4 or 5	SH	≤.90	AA	≤3.3	>.75	>5.58
Strong Short-Term Bond	4/5	SM	0.90	A	1.8	1.30	7.46
★Van F/I Sh-T Corporate	4/4	SM	0.25	A	2.6	0.99	7.01
William Blair Income	4/3	SH	0.70	AAA	4.8	0.82	7.20

Fund Category	(Ratings) Stars/ Category Rating	(Style) Current Style	(Costs) Expense Ratio	(Quality) Turnover Rate	(Risk) Beta vs. S&P 500	Sharpe Ratio	(Return) 3-Year Average Total Return
Intermediate Bond (5/23/97)							
Category average (385/20)	3/3	IH	0.93	AA	9.4	0.49	6.79
Desired standard	4 or 5	IH	≤.90	AA	≤9.4	>.75	>6.79
*Warburg Pincus Fxd Inc	4/5	IH	0.75	AA	7.2	1.31	8.81
Harbor Bond	4/4	IH	0.70	AA	8.1	1.02	9.13
Stein Roe Int Bond	4/4	IM	0.70	A	8.4	0.96	8.38
Columbia Fxd Inc Sec	4/4	IH	0.64	AA	5.9	0.88	8.52
Van Bond Index Total Mkt	4/4	IH	0.20	AA	8.7	0.87	8.40

Municipal Bond Funds

Fund Category	Stars/ Category Rating	Current Style	Expense Ratio	Turnover Rate	Beta vs. S&P 500	Sharpe Ratio	3-Year Average Total Return
Muni Short-Term (8/15/97)							
Category average (92/8)	4/3	SH	0.78	AA	4.1	−0.42	4.64
Desired standard	4 or 5	SH	≤.70	AA	≤4.1	>−.20	>4.64
Fid Sp S-Int Muni (10K)	5/4	SH	0.54	AA	3.4	−0.02	5.14
TR Price Tax-Free S-Int	5/4	SH	0.56	AA	3.7	−0.08	5.07
*Vanguard Muni Ltd-Term	5/4	SH	0.21	AA	3.2	−0.10	5.04
Muni National Intermediate (7/18/97)							
Category average (106/9)	4/3	IH	0.86	AA	8.2	0.34	6.00
Desired standard	4 or 5	IH	≤.80	AA	≤8.2	>.45	>6.00
Fid Ltd Term Muni Inc	5/4	IH	0.56	AA	7.7	0.57	7.12
*Vanguard Muni Int Term	5/4	IH	0.20	AA	6.9	0.49	6.65
Scudder M-T Tax-Free	5/3	IH	0.70	AA	6.8	0.49	6.69
Muni Single State Int (8/15/97)							
Category average (184/9)	3/3	IH	0.89	AA	9.3	0.24	5.81
Desired standard	4 or 5	IH	≤.85	AA	≤9.3	>.30	>5.81

Fund Category	Stars/ Category Rating (Ratings)	Current Style (Style)	Expense Ratio (Costs)	Turnover Rate (Quality)	Beta vs. S&P 500 (Risk)	Sharpe Ratio	3-Year Average Total Return (Return)
★Am Cen–Benham CA							
T-F Intermediate	4/4	IH	0.48	AA	8.3	0.47	6.56
Columbia (OR) Muni Bond[a]	4/4	IH	0.56	AA	13.1	0.44	6.62
★War Pinc NY Int Muni	4/4	SH	0.59	AA	4.8	0.26	5.67
Dreyfus NJ Int Muni Bond	3/3	IH	0.78	AA	7.7	0.26	6.06
Dreyfus FL Int Muni	3/2	IH	0.80	AAA	7.7	0.22	5.96

Notes: The dates in parentheses after each fund category are the publication dates for *Morningstar No-Load Funds* from which data for that category were taken.

The figures in parentheses after the category average are the total number of mutual funds in the category and the number covered in *Morningstar No-Load Funds,* respectively.

Minimum initial purchase requirements greater than $3,000 are shown after the fund name (e.g., 10K = $10,000).

Current styles for bond funds are SH Short-Term, High Quality; SM Short-Term, Medium Quality; IH Intermediate-Term, High Quality; IM Intermediate-Term, Medium Quality.

[a]Funds that did not meet all of the desired standards but were added to provide greater choice within a category.

Abbreviations Used in The Conover Short List

Am = America or American
Am Cen = American Century
Ben = Benham
Cap = Capital
Emg = Emerging
Ext = Extended
Fed = Federal
Fid Sp = Fidelity Spartan
Fxd Inc = Fixed Income
Gen = Genesis
G&I = Growth and Income
Govt = Government
Gr = Growth
Ind = Index
Int = Intermediate
Int'l = International

Longlf = Longleaf
Ltd = Limited
Mat = Maturity
Mkt = Market
M-T = Medium Term
Muni = Municipal
Neub & Berm = Neuberger & Berman
Ptrs = Partners
Sec = Securities
S-Int = Short Intermediate
S-T = Short-Term
T-F = Tax Free
Treas = Treasury
Van = Vanguard
War Pinc = Warburg Pincus

APPENDIX C

TOP-NOTCH MUTUAL FUND FAMILIES

Charles Schwab & Co., Inc.
101 Montgomery Street
San Francisco, CA 94104
800-435-4000
http://www.schwab.com

Fidelity Management &
　Research
82 Devonshire Street
Boston, MA 02109
800-544-8888
http://www.fidelity.com

The Vanguard Group
Vanguard Financial Center
P.O. Box 2600
Valley Forge, PA 19482
800-662-2739
http://www.vanguard.com

American Century–Benham
4500 Main Street
P.O. Box 419200
Kansas City, MO 64141-6200
800-345-2021

Columbia Funds Management
1301 S.W. Fifth Avenue
P.O. Box 1350
Portland, OR 97207-1350
800-547-1707

Dimensional Fund Advisors
1299 Ocean Avenue, 11th Floor
Santa Monica, CA 90401
310-395-8005

Dodge & Cox
One Sansome Street, 35th Floor
San Francisco, CA 94104
800-621-3979

Dreyfus
One Exchange Place
Boston, MA 02109
800-345-6561

Harbor Capital Advisors
One SeaGate
Toledo, OH 43666
800-422-1050

Harris Associates
(Oakmark Funds)
Two N. LaSalle Street
Chicago, IL 60602-3790
800-625-6275

INVESCO Funds Group
P.O. Box 173706
Denver, CO 80217-3706
800-525-8085

Janus Funds
100 Fillmore Street, Suite 300
Denver, CO 80206-4923
800-525-8983

Neuberger & Berman
605 Third Avenue, 2d Floor
New York, NY 10158-0006
800-877-9700

Nicholas Funds
700 N. Water Street, Suite 1010
Milwaukee, WI 53202
800-227-5987

T. Rowe Price Associates
100 E. Pratt Street
Baltimore, MD 21202
800-638-5660

Scudder Stevens & Clark
Two International Place
Boston, MA 02110
800-225-2470

Stein Roe & Farnham
P.O. Box 804058
Chicago, IL 60680
800-338-2550

Strong Capital Management
P.O. Box 2936
Milwaukee, WI 53201-2936
800-368-1030

Warburg Pincus Counsellors
466 Lexington Avenue
New York, NY 10017-3147
800-927-2874

APPENDIX D

MAGAZINES ON MUTUAL FUNDS

Smart Money
The Wall Street Journal Magazine of Personal Business
1790 Broadway
New York, NY 10019
800-444-4204 for subscriptions

Monthly magazine, $2.95 per issue—a must for the individual investor. Lots of good information about personal financial planning and mutual funds. My first choice.

Worth
Worth Reader Service
P.O. Box 55420
Boulder, CO 80322
800-777-1851 for subscriptions

Published monthly except Investing Guide in January and bimonthly in July/August—$3.00 per issue, $18.00 for a one-year subscription. One of the best. Lots of very useful information and perspective for the individual investor. Publishes an Annual Fund Guide, develops recommended portfolios, and identifies the 200 best financial advisers in America. My second choice after *Smart Money.*

Forbes
Forbes Subscriber Service
P.O. Box 37162
Boone, IA 50037-0162
800-888-9896

Twenty-seven issues per year—$5.00 per issue, $57.00 for annual subscription. Covers mutual funds investment trends. Publishes an annual mutual fund survey that ranks and rates funds and shows lots of relevant performance indicators. Uses information from Lipper Analytical Services and Morningstar. Worth reading to see how your funds compare.

Kiplinger's Personal Finance Magazine
Kiplinger Washington Editors, Inc.
Subscription Center/Customer Service
Editors Park, MD 20782
800-544-0155

Monthly magazine—$2.95 per issue, $19.95 for annual subscription. Frequently covers financial planning topics for individual investors and mutual funds. Publishes an annual mutual fund survey with pretty good data and rankings. Uses Micropal Data Inc. as its data source. Worth more for the accompanying articles than the rankings of over 2,000 funds.

Consumer Reports
Consumers Union of U.S., Inc.
101 Truman Avenue
Yonkers, NY 10703-1057
914-378-2000

Published monthly, and twice in December—$2.95 per issue, $24.00 for annual subscription. Focuses on a wide range of topics of interest to consumers. Published survey and rankings of funds that met established criteria in May 1997 issue. Data supplied by Morningstar. Typical no-nonsense approach to evaluation and reporting. Definitely worth buying this issue if you don't want an annual subscription.

Money
Money Customer Service
P.O. Box 670001
Tampa, FL 33660-0001
800-623-9970

Published monthly, except semimonthly in November—$39.89 per year. Published by Time-Life Inc., this is a good popular press magazine that has probably done a lot to increase the knowledge level of the general public on matters of personal finance. Often either shallow or a bit too glittery, but it published an excellent article on index funds in the January 1997 issue.

Mutual Funds
Institute for Econometric Research
2200 SW 10th Street
Deerfield Beach, FL 33442
800-442-9000

Published monthly—$2.50 per issue, $14.97 per year. Entire magazine devoted to mutual funds. Includes both articles and periodic surveys and ratings. Also assigns its own "all-star ratings" and provides one-page fund summaries of a few funds in each issue. Worth taking a look at an occasional issue, but not in the same league as *Worth, Smart Money,* or *Forbes.*

Fortune
Time & Life Building
Rockefeller Center
New York, NY 10020
800-621-8000 for subscriptions

Monthly magazine—$4.95 per issue. Outstanding business magazine, with articles and occasional surveys. Publishes an annual Investor's Guide at the start of each year. The 1997 and 1998 versions ranked funds in different groups according to their total return *after* loads and taxes, a significant contribution to the task of fund performance evaluation. Data provided by Morningstar. Even if you don't read *Fortune* regularly, it is definitely worth getting this one important issue.

Your Money
Consumers Digest, Inc.
P.O. Box 3084
Harlan, IA 51537-3084
800-777-0025 for subscriptions

Published bimonthly—$2.00 per issue, $15.97 per year. A consumer-oriented magazine with lots of articles on personal financial planning topics. Its "Mutual Fund Monitor" feature reports on mutual fund performance and includes the Morningstar ratings. Occasionally has a unique article or perspective, but does not measure up to the more popular choices.

Individual Investor
Subscription Fulfillment
P.O. Box 682
Mount Morris, IL 61054-0681
800-383-5901 for subscriptions

Monthly publication—$2.95 per issue. A glossy magazine that includes articles on more than just mutual funds. If you read my earlier choices, you can skip this one unless you see a particular article that sparks your interest.

GLOSSARY

12b-1 Fee: A method of charging distribution-related expenses directly against fund assets. The 12b-1 refers to the 1980 Securities and Exchange Commission rule authorizing these charges. These expenses are included in a fund's expense ratio.

401(k): A qualified retirement plan that allows employees of a company to contribute pretax earnings to a tax-deferred retirement plan. Generally, these plans offer their participants a variety of investment choices for their contributions. Earnings on contributions are tax deferred until withdrawal, when they are taxed at ordinary income tax rates. The Department of Labor establishes a ceiling for contributions each year that is subject to inflation increases. In 1998, the limit is $10,000.

403(b): A type of tax-sheltered annuity available to employees of the government and nonprofit organizations. Like a 401(k) plan, employees can make pretax contributions up to an annual limit—$10,000 in 1998.

Accumulation Period: The period during your working years when you make regular contributions to a deferred retirement or annuity account.

Active Management: Portfolio management that seeks to exceed the returns of the financial markets. Active managers rely on research, market forecasts, and their own experience in making investment decisions.

Adjusted Gross Income (AGI): An item shown on an individual's Form 1040, the level of AGI is used to determine eligibility for participation in certain individual retirement accounts and tax credits.

Aggressive Growth Fund: A mutual fund that seeks to provide maximum long-term capital growth from stocks of primarily smaller companies or narrow market segments. Any dividend income is incidental.

Alpha: The difference in percentage points between the actual return of a fund and its expected performance, given its volatility level (i.e., its beta). A positive alpha is considered a measure of the fund manager's contribution to the performance of the fund.

Annuity: A contract sold by an insurance company that provides a fixed or variable periodic payment to the annuitant. Contributions are made with after-tax dollars, and earnings are generally tax-deferred until withdrawals are made. Also, a stream of equal payments of principal and interest from an account until the principal is exhausted.

Asset: Property that you own that has monetary value. Assets can be tangible, such as homes, cars, and boats, or financial, such as stocks, bonds, and cash.

Asset Allocation: The process of deciding how your investment dollars should be apportioned among various classes of financial assets, such as stocks, bonds, and cash-equivalent assets. This selection can have a major impact on your long-term investment results.

Asset Class: Types of investments. The three primary classes are stocks, bonds, and cash. Other classes are designated by investment style (e.g. large-value) and specialty, such as technology or foreign.

Average Weighted Maturity: The length of time in days or years until the average security in a money market fund or bond fund will mature or be redeemed by its issuer. The average maturity is weighted according to the dollar amounts invested in the various securities in the fund. This measure indicates a fixed income fund's sensitivity to changes in interest rates. The longer the fund's average weighted maturity, the more its share price will fluctuate in response to changing interest rates.

Back-End Load: A sales commission assessed when an investor sells mutual fund shares. Also called a *redemption fee* or a *contingent deferred sales charge*. Some funds gradually phase out back-end loads over several years. You should avoid funds with back-end loads.

Balance Sheet: A financial statement listing all the owners' assets and liabilities, along with their values.

Balanced Fund: A mutual fund that seeks to provide both current income and long-term growth in principal and income by investing in a combination of stocks, bonds, and cash reserves.

Basis Point: One-hundredth of 1 percent. One percent equals 100 basis points; 40 basis points equals 0.40 percent.

Beta: A measure of how volatile a fund has been compared to an appropriate index, usually the Standard & Poor's 500. The index has a beta of 1.00. The price of a fund with a beta of 1.20 would be expected to rise or fall by 12 percent when the overall market rose or fell by 10 percent.

Bond: A security issued by a corporation or government entity in order to borrow money from investors. The borrower-issuer promises to pay interest at a fixed rate during the period that the bond is outstanding and to repay the principal in full at maturity. Bonds are issued for terms of up to 30 years or more.

Bond Fund: A mutual fund that invests in bonds—generally, corporate, municipal, or U.S. government debt obligations. Bond funds emphasize income rather than growth.

Bull Market: A market with a positive trend; it increases in value over an extended period of time.

Buy-and-Hold: A long-term investment strategy that emphasizes ignoring short-term market fluctuations and holding onto investments for an extended time period.

Call Risk: The possibility that bonds held by a mutual fund will be repaid or called prior to maturity. Issuers generally recall bonds when current interest rates are less than the rate on the bond being recalled. The risk is that you won't get the higher return for which you had hoped.

Capital Appreciation Fund: A mutual fund that seeks maximum appreciation by investing primarily in stocks. Another term for an aggressive growth fund.

Capital Gain/Loss: The difference between the sales price of a capital asset, such as a mutual fund, stock, or bond, and the cost basis of the asset. If the sales price is higher than the cost basis, there is a capital gain. If the sales price is lower than the cost basis, there is a capital loss.

Capital Gains Distributions: Payments made to mutual fund shareholders of profits from the sale of securities in the fund's portfolio. Capital gains distributions are generally made annually.

Capital Gains Tax: An income tax levied on the amount of capital gains realized by an investor. The level of the tax depends on how long the investor has owned the asset.

Capital Growth: An increase in the market value of a mutual fund's securities, reflected by the appreciation of its net asset value per share. Capital growth is a specific long-term objective for many stock mutual funds.

Capitalization: The total stock market value of a company's stock, determined by multiplying its price per share times the number of shares outstanding.

Cash-Equivalent Assets: Assets that can be readily converted to cash, such as short-term bank deposits, commercial paper, money market instruments, and U.S. Treasury bills. An investor is generally indifferent between holding these assets and holding cash.

Cash Reserves: Another term for cash-equivalent assets.

Certificates of Deposit (CD): A time deposit in a bank or thrift institution. The depositor receives interest from the bank and the face amount of the CD on its maturity date. Maturities range from weeks to several years, with the most common maturity being 1 year.

Closed Fund: An open-end mutual fund that is no longer accepting investments from new shareholders. Successful small-cap funds are often closed so that they will not be overwhelmed by new money, thus making it more difficult to maintain their good performance.

Closed-End Fund: A type of fund that has a fixed number of shares outstanding and is usually listed on a major stock exchange. Its price is determined by market forces, and it often sells at a discount from its net asset value.

Commercial Paper: Short-term debt obligations with maturities of up to 270 days issued by banks and corporations, and purchased by investors with temporarily idle cash. Normally issued only by top-rated concerns and often backed by bank lines of credit. Money market funds buy large amounts of commercial paper.

Commission: A fee paid to a broker for executing a trade. The amount is based on either the number of shares traded or the dollar amount of the trade.

Commodities: Bulk goods, such as grains, metals, and foods, traded on a commodities exchange.

Common Stock: A class of stock that carries voting rights and earns dividends. Common stockholders are the ultimate owners of a corporation and thus have the final claim on its assets and earnings.

Compound Interest: Interest earned on interest and capital gains that is retained and added to the principal of the investment; of great value to an investor.

Comptroller of the Currency: An agency of the federal government established in 1863 by President Lincoln. Today the Office of the Comptroller of the Currency (OCC) has nothing to do with currency. Rather, it supervises and regulates national banks. The OCC is responsible for chartering new banks, issuing regulations governing bank activities, examining them to ensure compliance with rules and regulations, taking enforcement actions against them when appropriate, and closing them when they become insolvent. The comptroller is appointed by the president and reports to the secretary of the treasury.

Consumer Price Index (CPI): A measure of the relative cost of living at any given time compared to a base year. Percentage changes in the CPI indicate the rate of inflation. The CPI is maintained by the Bureau of Labor Statistics, within the Department of Labor.

Contingent Deferred Sales Charge: Avoid them. *See* Back-End Load.

Cost Basis: For tax purposes, the original cost of an investment, including any reinvested dividends and capital gains distributions. The cost basis is subtracted from the selling price to determine any capital gain or loss from the sale of mutual fund shares or other securities.

Credit Quality: A measure of a bond issuer's ability to repay interest and principal in a timely manner.

Credit Rating: A published rating, based on careful financial analysis, of a creditor's ability to pay interest and principal on a debt. Ratings are provided by Moody's and Standard & Poor's.

Credit Risk: The possibility that a bond issuer will default (i.e., fail to make interest and principal payments in a timely manner). Also known as *default-risk.*

Currency Risk: The potential for price fluctuations in the dollar value of international stocks due to changing currency exchange rates. A stronger dollar (and a decline in local currency) reduces the dollar value of foreign stocks.

Defined Benefit Plan: A retirement plan, often known as a pension plan, that guarantees a certain benefit, usually based on average salary prior to retirement and number of years of service.

Defined Contribution Plan: A retirement plan offering a benefit that depends on the contributions made by the employee and the employer and on the investment returns earned on those contributions. In these plans, employees bear the investment risk.

Discount Broker: A brokerage firm that executes buy and sell orders at lower commission rates than those charged by a full-service broker, and may not offer all the services provided by a full-service broker. Schwab, Fidelity, Vanguard, and Jack White all operate as discount brokers.

Diversify, Diversification: A strategy for investing in different asset classes in order to reduce the risk inherent in investing in a single class.

Dividend: A distribution of earnings to investors who own stock in a company or shares in a mutual fund. Mutual fund dividends may include earnings from interest or dividends on stocks held by the fund. Depending on the type of mutual fund, dividends may be paid monthly, quarterly, semiannually, or annually.

Dividend Yield: The current annualized rate of dividends paid on a share of stock, divided by its current share price. For a portfolio, the weighted average yield on stocks it holds.

Dollar-Cost Averaging: The technique of investing a fixed sum at regular intervals regardless of financial market movements. This strategy minimizes the risk by reducing the average share cost to the investor who acquires more shares in periods of lower prices and fewer shares when prices are high.

Dow-Jones Industrial Average (DJIA): An index that tracks the daily share of 30 large U.S. companies that are leaders in their respective sectors. Widely quoted as an indicator of how the market performs each day. The S&P 500 Index, which tracks 500 companies, is more representative of the broad U.S. market.

Duration: A mathematical calculation of the average life of a bond or bond fund that serves as a useful measure of the sensitivity of bond prices to changes in interest rates. Each year of duration represents an expected 1 percent change in the price of a bond for every 1 percent change in interest rates. For example, if a bond fund has an average duration of 3 years, its price will fall about 3 percent when interest rates rise by one percentage point. Conversely, the bond fund's price will rise by about 3 percent when interest rates fall by one percentage point.

Earned Income: Compensation earned for providing a service—for example, wages, salaries, tips, alimony, compensation, and net self-employed income.

Earnings Growth Rate: The average annual rate of growth in earnings over the past 3 to 5 years for the stocks now held in a portfolio.

Earnings per Share (EPS): A company's total earnings after taxes divided by the number of common shares outstanding.

Emerging Markets Fund: A mutual fund that invests primarily in developing countries. Emerging market funds tend to be volatile, so values can fluctuate dramatically.

Employer Matching Contribution: The amount, if any, that a company contributes on an employee's behalf to his or her retirement account, such as a 401(k) plan. For example, a company might make a matching contribution equal to 50 percent of the employee's contributions up to a maximum of 6 percent of his or her salary. In that case, the matching contribution would be 3 percent of the employee's salary.

Equities: A synonym for *common stocks*. Those who own the equity of a company own the company and are entitled to its residual profits after all its expenses, including interest payments and income taxes, have been paid.

Estate Planning: The preparation of a plan, and any related documents, to carry out an individual's wishes regarding the administration and distribution of property before or after his or her death. Common elements of an estate plan are a will, a power of attorney, and trusts.

Estate Tax: A tax imposed on the right to transfer property at death. Thus, an estate tax is levied on the decedent's estate and not the heir who is receiving property. Individual retirement account assets may be included in the estate and be subject to the estate tax.

Expense Ratio: The percentage of a fund's average net assets used to pay fund expenses. The expenses included in the calculation include account management fees, administrative costs, and any 12b-1 fees. These expenses directly reduce returns to shareholders.

Fixed Income Fund: A mutual fund with the objective of providing current income from fixed income securities.

Fixed Income Securities: Another name for bonds or other securities that provide current income from a fixed schedule of interest payments.

Front-End Load: A sales commission, or load, paid when shares of a mutual fund are purchased.

Fund Assets: The total value of a portfolio's securities, cash, and other holdings, minus any outstanding debts.

Global Fund: A mutual fund that invests in both U.S. and foreign securities.

GNMA (Government National Mortgage Association): An agency within the U.S. Department of Housing and Urban Development that buys mortgages from lending institutions and pools them to form securities, which it then sells to investors. A mutual fund that invests in such securities is known as a GNMA ("Ginnie Mae") fund.

Growth Fund: A mutual fund whose main objective is long-term growth in capital from stocks.

Growth Investing: A strategy for equity investing that emphasizes stocks with above-average price/earnings and price/book ratios and sales and earnings growth, but below-average dividend yields. It is an approach typically followed by investors seeking long-term growth.

Growth Stocks: Stocks of companies that have experienced rapid growth in revenue or earnings per share and are expected to continue such growth for an extended period in the future. Such stocks typically have relatively low dividend yields and sell at relatively high prices in relation to their earnings and book value. Mutual funds that emphasize such stocks are known as *growth funds.*

Growth and Income Fund: A mutual fund whose aim is to provide long-term growth of principal and income, and current dividend income from stocks.

Income: Interest and dividends earned on securities held by a mutual fund and paid out to fund shareholders in the form of income dividends.

Income Dividend: Payments to fund shareholders of dividends and interest earned by securities held by a mutual fund. Paid after deducting operating expenses.

Income Fund: A mutual fund that seeks current income rather than growth of capital. Such funds typically invest in bonds and/or high-yielding stocks.

Index: An indicator that reflects the value of a representative grouping of securities. The S&P 500 Index is a good example of a domestic stock index.

Index Fund: A mutual fund that invests in a portfolio of securities designed to match the performance of a given index, such as the S&P 500.

Index Investing: An investment strategy involving the creating of a portfolio tailored as closely as possible to match the investment performance of a specific stock or bond index and thus expected to provide a highly predictable return relative to specific benchmarks. Index funds offer investors the advantage of a "passive" approach to investing: low costs, tax efficiency, exceptional diversification, low turnover, and relative predictability.

Individual Retirement Account (IRA): A tax-advantaged savings plan for workers that allows annual contributions of up to $2,000 per person. There are two kinds of IRAs for retirement: the traditional IRA and the Roth IRA.

Inflation: An increase in the prices of goods and services. If something that a year ago cost $15.00 now costs $16.50, inflation has been 10 percent. For the nation as a whole it is measured by changes in Consumer Price Index, compiled and maintained by the Bureau of Labor Statistics.

Inflation Risk: The possibility that increases in the cost of living will reduce or eliminate the returns on a particular investment, usually a fixed income investment.

Interest Rate Risk: The risk that a security or mutual fund will decline in value because of increases in market interest rates.

Intermediate-Term Bonds: Bonds with maturities of more than 4 but less than 10 years. These bonds are likely to have durations of at least 3.5 years and no more than 6 years.

International Fund: A mutual fund that invests in securities traded in markets outside the United States.

Invest, Investing: To put the money that you have saved to work so that it will increase in value through a combination of income dividends, capital gains distributions, and unrealized share appreciation.

Investment Horizon: The length of time that you expect to keep a sum of money invested (e.g., the 20 years between now and your planned retirement date).

Investment Objective: The financial goal that an investor or mutual fund pursues. A growth fund, for example, typically seeks to provide long-term growth as opposed to current income.

Keogh Plan: A retirement plan (also known as an H.R. 10 Plan) that permits unincorporated self-employed individuals to set aside savings for retirement. The self-employed person may contribute up to 15 percent of gross self-employed income, to an annual limit of $30,000. Contributions are deductible, and earnings on them are tax deferred until withdrawals are made at retirement.

Large Capitalization Stocks: The stocks of companies whose aggregate market value (i.e., shares outstanding × price per share) is more than $5 billion.

Liability: An amount owed, such as the outstanding balance on a mortgage or credit card, or the principal or interest to be paid by a bond issuer.

Life Expectancy: The age to which an average person is expected to live, as calculated by actuaries. Life expectancy is affected by many factors, including age, gender, heredity, and health characteristics.

Liquidity: How quickly an investment can be turned into cash. A mutual fund, for example, is usually a very liquid investment because shares can be redeemed at any time. In contrast, a house or a parcel of land is a very illiquid investment.

Load: A sales charge or commission assessed by certain mutual funds ("load funds") to cover their selling costs. Loads range from 1.0 to 8.5 percent of the amount invested.

Load Fund: A mutual fund that levies a sales charge. *See* Back-End Load; Front-End Load.

Long-Term Bonds: Bonds with a remaining maturity of more than 10 years and a duration of more than 6 years.

Long-Term Capital Gains: A profit on the sale of a security or mutual fund that has been held for 12 to 18 months and is subject to a 28 percent federal tax, or more than 18 months and subject to a 20 percent capital gains tax.

Low-Load Fund: A mutual fund that charges a sales commission of 3.5 percent or less for the purchase of its shares.

Management Fee: The amount a mutual fund pays to its investment adviser for the investment management associated with overseeing the fund's portfolio. Usually expressed as a percentage of net assets (e.g., 0.75 percent of net assets).

Marginal Tax Rate: The income tax rate at which the last dollar of income is taxed. Under federal law, a lower rate is paid on the first dollar of income than on the last dollar. The marginal rate—the highest rate at which income is taxed—should be used to evaluate potential taxes due on investment income.

Market Capitalization: The total value of all a company's or fund's outstanding shares, calculated by multiplying the market price per share (the net asset value for mutual funds) times the number of shares outstanding.

Market Risk: The possibility that stock or bond prices will fluctuate.

Market Timing: An investment strategy based on predicting market trends. The goal is to anticipate market trends, buying before the market goes up and selling before it goes down. The results over the long term have been less successful with this type of strategy than with the buy-and-hold strategy.

Market Value: The total number of company stock shares multiplied by the price per share; also, the amount that an investor could get for an asset by selling it in the marketplace today.

Maturity: The date on which payment of a financial obligation, such as a bond, is due. An investor who buys $10,000 worth of 20-year bonds will receive $10,000 at the end of 20 years, after having received interest payments over the 20-year period. Also, the number of years or months from the present to the maturity date.

Median Market Cap: The middle stock, in terms of market capitalization (market price × shares outstanding), in a portfolio or mutual fund.

Mid-Cap Funds: Companies or funds that have median market capitalizations in the $1 billion to $5 billion range.

Money Market Fund: A mutual fund that invests in short-term, high-quality securities such as Treasury bills, negotiable certificates of deposit, and commercial paper. Net asset values are maintained at $1 per share. Returns reflect short-term interest rates. They are very liquid and safe. Yields vary only slightly among different funds.

Municipal Bond Fund: A mutual fund that invests in tax-exempt bonds issued by state, city, and local governments. The interest obtained from these bonds is passed through to shareholders and is generally free of federal, state, and local income taxes.

Mutual Fund: An investment company that combines the money of thousands of people and invests it in a variety of securities in an effort to achieve a specific financial objective over time. An open-end mutual fund stands ready to buy back its shares at the then-current net asset value.

National Association of Securities Dealers (NASD): Organization of brokers and dealers set up to protect the investing public against fraudulent acts; administers rules of fair practice.

National Association of Securities Dealers Automated Quotations (NASDAQ): A system that provides price quotations for securities traded over the counter as well as for many New York Stock Exchange-listed securities.

Net Asset Value (NAV): The price of each mutual fund share, determined at the end of each trading day by dividing the total value of the fund's investments by the number of shares that the fund has outstanding. Thus, a fund that owns $200 million worth of stocks, bonds, and cash equivalents and has 4 million shares owned by its investors has a NAV of $50.00.

Net Worth: The total value of an individual's assets, less the value of any outstanding debts (i.e., liabilities). Net worth is the measure of an individual's material wealth.

New York Stock Exchange (NYSE): The oldest (since 1792) and largest stock exchange in the U.S. located at 11 Wall Street in New York City. The NYSE is an unincorporated association governed by a board of directors headed by a full-time paid chairman and comprising 20 individuals representing the public and the exchange membership in about equal proportions.

No-Load Fund: A mutual fund that sells its shares at net asset value, without charging a sales commission, or load. Funds that are sold without 12b-1 fees or any sales loads are called *pure no-load funds* or *true no-load funds*.

Normal Retirement Age: The age at which a participant in social security or a private pension plan is eligible for full retirement benefits.

Passive Management: An investment management approach that seeks to match the return and risk characteristics of a discrete market segment, or index, by holding all the securities that compose the market segment or a statistically representative sample of the index.

Pension Plan: A qualified retirement plan established by an employer for its employees. Types of pension plans include profit-sharing plans, stock bonus plans, thrift plans, target benefit plans, money purchase plans, defined benefit plans, and employee stock ownership plans.

Portfolio: All the securities held by a mutual fund; a term for describing all the investments that you own (stocks, bonds, mutual funds, cash-equivalent assets). A diversified portfolio contains a variety of investments with different characteristics.

Portfolio Diversification: Holding a variety of securities so that a portfolio's return is not hurt by the poor performance of a single security, industry, or country.

Portfolio Manager: The individual responsible for managing a mutual fund's assets.

Portfolio Transaction Costs: The costs associated with buying and selling securities, including commissions on trades, dealer markups on bonds, bid-ask spreads, and any other miscellaneous expenses. These costs are not included in the expense ratio that funds report.

Prepayment Risk: The possibility that as interest rates fall, homeowners will refinance their home mortgages resulting in the prepayment of GNMA securities.

Price/Book Ratio: The price per share of a stock divided by its book value (i.e., net worth) per share. For a portfolio, the ratio is the weighted average price/book ratio of the stocks it holds.

Price/Earnings Ratio: The ratio of a stock's current price to its earnings per share over the past year. For a portfolio, the ratio is the weighted average P/E of the stocks it holds. P/E is an indicator of market expectations about corporate prospects; the higher the P/E, the greater the expectations for a company's future growth in earnings.

Principal: The amount of your own money that your originally put into an investment.

Profit-Sharing Plan: A defined contribution plan in which contributions, based on each participant's compensation, can be varied and no minimum contribution is required. An employer may still contribute to a profit-sharing plan even if there are no profits.

Prospectus: A legal document providing pertinent information about a mutual fund, including discussions of the fund's investment objectives and policies, risks, costs, past performance, and other information useful to prospective investors.

Qualified Retirement Plan: A plan that meets the requirement of Internal Revenue Code Section 401(a) and is eligible for special tax considerations. For example, employers can deduct plan contributions made on behalf of eligible employees on the business' tax return as business expenses, and earnings on plan assets are not taxed until they are distributed.

R-squared: A measure of how much of a portfolio's past returns can be explained by the returns from the overall market (or its benchmark index). If a portfolio's return were precisely synchronized with the overall market return, its R-squared would be 1.0; if the return bore no relationship to the market's returns, its R-squared would be 0.0.

Real Return: The actual return received on an investment after factoring in the rate of inflation. For example, if the nominal investment return for a particular period is 8 percent and inflation is 3 percent, the real return is 5 percent. Also known as the *inflation-adjusted return*.

Risk: The potential to lose money (principal and any earnings) or not to make money on an investment.

Risk Tolerance: An investor's personal ability or willingness to endure fluctuations, especially declines, in the prices of investments.

Rollover: A tax-free transfer of cash or other assets from one retirement plan to another. An individual retirement account (IRA) holder may shift assets from his or her current IRA to another. Distributions from a qualified retirement plan may also be rolled over to an IRA or to another employer's plan.

Rollover Individual Retirement Account (IRA): IRA established for the sole purpose of receiving a distribution from another qualified plan.

Russell 2000 Index: The most commonly used benchmark for small-cap investments. It tracks the returns of the smallest 2,000 companies in the Russell 3000 Index, which measures the 3,000 companies with the largest market capitalization in the United States.

Save, Saving: To divert money from a spending plan and invest it so that it will grow to a larger amount in the future.

Schwab 1000: An index that tracks the returns of the 1,000 largest publicly traded companies in the United States.

Schwab Small-Cap Index: An index that tracks the returns of the second largest 1,000 U.S. companies.

S&P/BARRA Growth Index: An index that tracks the returns of the most expensive half of the S&P 500 Index, as measured by the price/book ratio.

S&P/BARRA Value Index: An index that tracks the returns of the least expensive half of the S&P 500 Index, as measured by the price/book ratio.

Sector Fund: A mutual fund that concentrates its investments in a particular industry or market sector.

Securities and Exchange Commission (SEC): The federal government agency that regulates mutual funds, registered investment advisers, the stock and bond markets, and securities broker-dealers. Established by Congress, it protects investors against malpractice in the securities markets.

Self-Employed Individual: A sole proprietor or a partner in a partnership.

Share: A unit of equity ownership in a corporation, represented by a stock certificate, which names the company and the share owner. Also a unit of ownership in a mutual fund.

Short-Term Capital Gain: A profit on the sale of a security or mutual fund held for 1 year or less.

Simplified Employee Pension (SEP-IRA): A retirement program that takes the form of individual retirement accounts for all eligible employees and is subject to special rules on contributions and eligibility.

Small Capitalization Stock: The stock of companies whose market value is less than $1 billion. Small-cap companies grow faster than large-cap companies and typically use any profits for expansion rather than for paying dividends. They are also more volatile than large-cap companies and fail more often.

Split: The board of directors of a corporation increases the total number of shares outstanding. The increase in the number of shares results in a decline in share price. For example, if a company declares a "3 for 1" stock split and the price of the stock is currently $60 per share, a shareholder with 100 shares before the split would have 300 shares after the split with a value of $20 per share. The shareholders' equity does not change.

Standard Deviation: The percentage range that a fund's monthly returns have deviated from its average or mean return. The larger the standard deviation, the more volatile the fund. While beta measures a fund's volatility relative to the S&P 500, standard deviation measures a fund's pure volatility based on the consistency of its own monthly returns.

Standard & Poor's (S&P) 500: An index of the largest, most actively traded stocks on the New York Stock Exchange. It provides a guide to the overall health of the U.S. stock market. The S&P 500 is a much broader index than the Dow Jones Industrial Average and reflects the stock market more accurately.

Stock: Security that represents part ownership, or equity, in a corporation. Each share of stock is a claim on its proportionate stake in the corporation's assets and profits, some of which may be paid out as dividends.

Stock Fund: A mutual fund whose holdings consist mainly of stocks.

Tax-Deferred Retirement Plan: Any retirement plan in which earnings are not currently taxable.

Tax-Exempt Bond: A bond whose interest payments are not subject to income tax. Bonds issued by municipal, county, and state governments and agencies typically are federally tax exempt and may also be exempt from state or local income taxes. Also known as *municipal bonds* or *tax-free bonds*.

Tax-Exempt Income Fund: Mutual funds that attempt to provide the highest level of income exempt from federal income tax, consistent with preservation of capital and each portfolio's risk characteristics.

Total Return: Dividend or interest income plus any capital gains divided by beginning asset value with the answer expressed as an annual percentage rate. Total return is the best overall measure of fund performance. This measure is reported in most newspapers and other periodicals.

Treasury bill (T-bill): A short-term discounted security issued by the government, with a maturity of from 90 to 364 days. T-bills have a face value and sell at a discount based at current rates. The yield on a T-bill is often referred to as the *risk-free yield*.

Trust: A legal arrangement in which a fiduciary, or trustee, holds title to assets (e.g., investments, real estate) for the benefit of another person or persons (the beneficiaries).

Turnover Rate: The percentage rate at which a fund buys and sells securities each year. For example, if a fund's assets total $100 million and the fund bought and sold $100 million worth of securities that year, its portfolio turn-over rate would be 100 percent.

Unified Tax Credit: A federal tax credit that may be applied against the gift tax and estate tax. Each individual is entitled to a credit sufficient to shelter $625,000 in 1998 assets from estate taxes. The amount gradually increases until the credit will shelter $1 million in 2006.

Uniform Gifts/Transfer to Minors Act: A form of account registration in which a custodian acts on behalf of a beneficial owner who is a minor. Such accounts are often referred to by their acronyms: UGMA or UTMA.

Value Investing: A strategy for equity investing that emphasizes stocks with below-average price-to-book ratios but above-average dividend yields. It may be appropriate for conservative investors seeking dividend income (e.g., those in their retirement years).

Value Stocks: Stocks that have relatively high dividend yields and sell at relatively low prices in relation to their earnings or book value.

Vesting: Represents a nonforfeitable interest of a participant in his or her account balance under a defined contribution plan or in his or her accrued benefit under a defined benefit plan.

Volatility: The fluctuations in market value of a mutual fund or other security. The greater a fund's volatility, the wider the fluctuations between its high and low prices, and the higher its standard deviation.

Withdrawal: Taking money out of a tax-advantaged retirement plan, which makes it subject to a possible penalty if the individual is under the age of 59$^{1}/_{2}$.

Wilshire 4500: An index that tracks the performance of the 4,500 largest U.S. companies outside of the S&P 500 Index.

Wilshire 5000: An index that measures returns of 5,000 of the largest U.S. stocks, measured by market capitalization. Since it is one of the broadest in-dexes, it is considered to track the returns of all U.S. stocks.

Yield: Income received from investments, usually expressed as a percentage of a fund's share price.

Yield to Maturity: A concept used to determine the rate of return an investor will receive if a long-term credit instrument, such as a bond, is held until its maturity date.

Zero Coupon Bond: A security that makes no payment of interest. Instead, the bond is sold at a deep discount from its face vale. The interest paid on the bond is the difference between its discounted price and the full face value of the bond, which is paid to the bondholder on a specified maturity date.

INDEX

About the Author

C. Todd Conover, an individual investor and private investment adviser, is also president of the Vantage Group, a consulting firm headquartered in Los Altos, California. He works with clients in the financial services industry on problems involving strategy, marketing, and profit improvement.

He has nearly 30 years of experience as a consultant, regulator, and bank executive. Mr. Conover's consulting experience includes stints with McKinsey & Company; Edgar, Dunn & Company, where he was a founding partner, and KPMG Peat Marwick, where he was national director of bank consulting. He has also been president and CEO of a $2.5 billion bank holding company with 35 branches.

During the Reagan administration, he was the U.S. Comptroller of the Currency. Appointed by the president, he managed an organization of 3,000 people and was the principal regulator of over 4,500 national banks. He was also one of three directors in the Federal Deposit Insurance Corporation.

He serves on the board of directors of two large public companies: PacifiCorp, a $14 billion international energy company headquartered in Portland, Oregon, and Blount International, a diversified industrial company headquartered in Montgomery, Alabama, and listed on the New York Stock Exchange. He is also a director of Tracy Federal Bank, a community bank in Tracy, California, and a member of the advisory board of the California Community Financial Institutions Fund, sponsored by Belvedere Capital Partners.

He received his B.A. from Yale University and an M.B.A. in finance from the University of California at Berkeley.